Creative Dramatics
and
English Teaching

Creative Dramatics and English Teaching

Charles R. Duke

National Council of Teachers of English
1111 Kenyon Road, Urbana, Illinois 61801

Library of Congress Catalog Card Number 74-81362
NCTE Stock Number 01223

Second Printing

Contents

Introduction

The classroom is strangely silent; clusters of students, their eyes closed, walk cautiously around the room, their outstretched hands brushing against desks, chairs, people, and space. Gradually students begin to leave the room, but only after they have touched each other to make sure they are not alone. Occasional light tapping sounds, the noise of scuffing feet, and the sound of a few muffled giggles float back into the classroom through the open door. Passers-by in the hallway stop in astonishment to see this strange activity. "What's happening?" a passing teacher inquires of another. "Oh," the other teacher responds, "That's Mr. D's class; they're exploring their environment without the benefit of sight as a part of their study of *The Miracle Worker;* they take turns guiding each other without the benefit of verbal directions; Mr. D says it's all part of something called creative dramatics."

Pairs of students begin to return to the classroom; once everyone is present and eyes are open, the comments begin. "Gee, that was weird—I never felt so alone in all my life. I was sure glad that if I had to, I could open my eyes and know where I was." The discussion of their experiences continues with excitement and wonder. What had seemed so remote from their experience a few minutes ago is now a real part of their minds. Helen Keller's helplessness and her attempts to make her way in the world are now much closer to students as a result of direct, dramatic experience.

The scene shifts. Tony and Meg are having trouble in their writing course with point of view; the usual explanations of first person central, third person omniscient have been read and discussed; still, some confusion remains. Today, as class begins, Tony and Meg have been talking between themselves about the problem and have agreed to bring it up in class once again. "Mr. D, we're still not sure of how we go about using point of view in our writing." Mr. D pauses for a moment and then asks Meg, "What's your point of view about streakers?" Meg, taken aback, finally says, "Why, I guess it's OK if people want to go around naked but it seems kind of primitive, you know, but it's just a fad, you know, and it's got to the point where people don't even pay much attention anymore."

The teacher nods his head and then asks the same question of Tony; he replies that he agrees with Meg. Mr. D asks several other students, who offer varying points of view on the subject of streaking. After this discussion, the teacher outlines the following situation. Pat, a college student from a small town, has just been caught and arrested for streaking; free on bail, she has gone home to await trial. In the meantime, her family has read about the escapade in the local newspaper and is awaiting her arrival.

At this point, Mr. D invites volunteers from the class to assign themselves various roles, including those of Pat, her father, mother, brother, sister, and the family minister. Students are to improvise the dialogue and action they think would occur when Pat arrives home. After a quick huddle, they push some desks around to suggest some physical boundaries and then begin the action. The first few minutes are awkward, but then the dialogue becomes more spirited as the boy playing the father begins to scold Pat for her actions. The players slip into their roles quite easily and the pace picks up. At the height of the verbal battle between Pat and her father, one of the players breaks character and exclaims in astonishment, "Hey, you can really get involved in this, can't you." Stopping the action at this point, the teacher turns to the students who have been watching the scene and asks them to think about how they would tell a reader what happened in the confrontation between the family and Pat and who they think is the most important character.

After a moment, suggestions begin to pop up all over the room. "I think the story should focus on Pat 'cause she's the one in trouble." Another student exclaims, "No, the father and the mother are the real important ones because they're the ones who have to pay the court costs and besides, they brought Pat up and look what's happened." In the midst of the debate, the teacher begins to probe a bit further: "OK, so Pat is the center of the story; Tony—how are you going to make the reader see the story through Pat's eyes?"

Tony, who up to now has been quiet but intent upon the action, says, "Oh, yeah—Pat's got to tell the story if we really want to see it from her point of view." He suddenly pauses and then with a sheepish grin says, "Point of view—geez, there it is." The discussion continues, centering upon the relationships among the characters and what adjustments would have to be made if the minister tells the story, or if the author wants the reader to know what is going on in the minds of all the characters. At the end of the class, Mr. D asks the students what the difference is between the first discussion they had about streaking and the one they just finished. A student points out that in the first discussion they were talking about someone's point of view, but in terms of his opinion. After the scene was dramatized, they were talking about who was going to tell the story and how much the reader was going to be allowed to know. Once again, creative dramatics had helped to clarify an idea through direct participation and dramatic involvement.

Recent conferences at Dartmouth College (1966), Vancouver, British Columbia (1967), and York, England (1971) have shown a growing awareness of the need for creative change in the teaching of English. Although this developing awareness is not a new phenomenon, its emergence at this time seems most significant. In a world where rapid social and intellectual changes are becoming commonplace, a growing need is apparent for greater adaptability and flexibility. The corresponding interest now appearing in the call for greater use of creative expression in education is a response to this need. Schools are trying to place greater emphasis upon student participation and an awareness of individual differences, but at the same time society is also calling for increased accountability and closer attention to behavior in education. Caught in the middle of these demands, education must find ways to balance the call for more attention to cognitive behavior with the equally desirable attention to affective behavior.

Creative expression and drama play important roles in leading education toward a more humanistic approach to learning as well as toward the development of students who are capable of responding more rationally to their changing world. Many educators have ignored the need for balance between the affective and the cognitive in the educational process. For years educators have given lip service to the fostering of creativity, but the creative process has remained something of a mystery, and few opportunities are presented to students regularly in which creative expression is allowed.

But one particular aspect of drama in education, that of creative dramatics, offers a means for solving this problem. Consequently, it is the purpose of this book to focus on certain concrete suggestions for implementing creative dramatic techniques. For ease in use, the book is divided into three sections. Part One discusses the theoretical background concerning the creative process, the development of children's drama, the relationship between creative dramatics and the development of the child, special areas and applications of drama in education, and the future of creative dramatics. Part Two deals with the role of the teacher in fostering creative expression, particularly through the use of creative dramatics, and suggests methods for guiding students in creative dramatic activities. Part Three provides a handbook of resources for creative dramatics.

It is not the intent of *Creative Dramatics and English Teaching* to provide a definitive examination of drama in the schools; instead, it is hoped that teachers unfamiliar with the role of creative dramatics will find specific help in understanding what can be done with this technique; for the experienced teacher, the book provides up-to-date listings of sources for materials, suggested activities that may have been overlooked, and, most importantly, a reassurance that creative expression and dramatic activity are integral to any educational program.

At this time I would like to acknowledge the contributions of several people to this work. I am particularly indebted to R. Baird Shuman of Duke University who encouraged and guided me in the development of this book. Particular thanks also go to Richard Sanderson of Plymouth State College who has often served as a sounding board for my ideas and theories. I also thank my wife Jonquelyn for her patience and understanding during the long hours of research, writing, and rewriting. And finally, but most importantly, my appreciation to all my students who have, by their responses, shown how important drama is to our lives.

C. R. D.

Plymouth State College
Plymouth, New Hampshire

PART ONE

Creativity, Drama, and Education

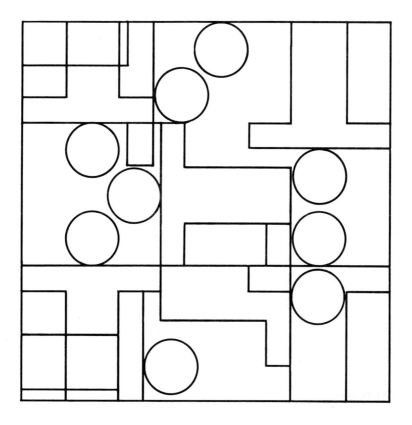

1 The Role of Creative Expression in Education

The urge to question, to invent, and to perform has been stifled in millions of schoolchildren now grown up, and their final cultural pattern can be seen all around us. But within this culture which in the past has tended toward rigidity, there are now definite needs for adaptability to rapid social change and a flexibility which will allow us to cope with problems yet to appear. Ours is a society which is finding habits, precedents, and traditions insufficient to guide and set courses for the future. For this reason alone we need, more than ever before, to place a higher priority upon the development of creative expression.

We cannot think of what our world calls for without realizing that today it is most important to stimulate the creative. That has not always been the aim of education. In some civilizations, as in the Chinese education of the past, the aim was to memorize, to follow the past, to insure conformity. In contrast, in all aspects of education today, there is an urgent need for the creative. [1]

But "creativity" tends to be a political word; to many individuals, favoring creativity means that one has to be automatically in favor of a variety of obscure though greatly ennobling educational alternatives and opposed to such things as programmed learning and science. Such an interpretation merely highlights the confusion which surrounds the whole concept of creativity, for a good part of the reaction to the term stems from the fact that no one seems exactly certain what creativity is, although countless definitions have been offered. For example, creativity could be defined as "taking known bits of information and putting them together in a way that no one else has thought of before." [2] Or we might turn to the field of psychology and claim that

3

"creativity is the idiosyncratic perception of new intellectual relationships never before experienced by the individual between two or more stimuli."[3] We might also, if we wished, point out that there are different types of creativity which seem to appear at special times. I. A. Taylor suggests that we should think of creativity in terms of various levels such as the following:

1. *Expressive creativity*—independent expression where skills, originality, and the quality of the product are unimportant, as in the spontaneous drawing of children.

2. *Productive creativity*—artistic or scientific production where there is a tendency to restrict and control free play and develop techniques for producing finished products.

3. *Inventive creativity*—invention, exploration, and discovery, where ingenuity is displayed with materials, methods, and techniques.

4. *Innovative creativity*—improvement through modification involving conceptualizing skills.

5. *Emergentive creativity*—development of an entirely new principle or assumption around which new schools flourish.[4]

But no matter what approach we take in defining the term, running through all the definitions seems to be a common denominator—the role of the imagination. There is, of course, some confusion about imagination as well. Many people think it is independent of reality—another name for fantasy. Actually, a person is imaginative in his efforts to assemble and recreate what he believes is fact. So although we may not completely understand yet the exact role that imagination plays in the mind's creative activity, we can recognize that the linking of the imagination and creative expression is important, for "imagination is the quality of the mind and spirit that enables one to understand experience beyond his own."[5]

Normally when one thinks of creative expression and the imagination, he will point to the arts as offering the best examples of what that combination can accomplish, since all art begins in the imagination and is then communicated by an effort of the will through various means of expression. These means may manifest themselves in painting, music, writing, drama, or some other form. Even the play of a small child which starts as a simple activity with no expressed content can be gradually filled with subject matter and thus move toward artistic creation.[6] According to E. G. Schactel, "The main motivation at the root of creative experience is man's need to relate to the world around him. . . . This need is apparent in the young child's interest in all the objects around him and his ever renewed explorations of and play with them."[7] Hence, to sense the satisfaction of original expression and to feel one's own worth and human potentiality are valid reasons why every human being should learn to value his creative abilities.

Viktor Lowenfeld and W. Lambert Brittain suggest, though, that "the ability to question, to seek answers, to find form and order, to rethink and restructure and find new relationships, are qualities that are generally not taught."[8] Although the structure of education does tend to minimize as much as possible the role of originality and fluency in thought, contemporary learning theories place a premium on the learning stimuli which young children receive from being free to explore unknown situations and to accept and seek challenges which call into play freshly won skills and understanding.[9] This living at the constantly changing edge of learning-potential fosters the expression of creativity and the development of the individual.

Creativity has often come close to being a lost cause in American education. Progressive education, a phenomenon which has been observed only rarely in its pure form, helped to revive its spirit in the 1920s and 1930s; in subsequent years creative expression has been both in and out of fashion with educators. Although the general public has not always recognized the need for creativity, at the present time pressures are being exerted on the educational system which, in essence, condemn traditional teaching methods. What is being called for is a reorganization of content, a redefining of the purposes of education, and a generalized demand for greater individualization of instruction. All of these challenges invite a greater recognition of the creative processes in education. The schools are also pressured to educate for creative expression because it is becoming increasingly evident that not only mankind's progress but his very survival may depend upon the creative ability that he brings to a world being made, paradoxically, both larger and smaller by science and technology. And certainly if we are to concern ourselves with an education for reality—a demand that society seems to be making more and more insistently—then we must concern ourselves with the inner world of the individual as well as with his outer world. Young children tend to make the transition between the inner and outer worlds easily, and they intuitively use symbolism such as language in the pursuit of an inward strength and an adequate sense of reality.[10] It is one of the tasks of education to insure that this transitional process remains free to operate as the individual matures. To do this calls for a fostering of creative expression, for through self-expression comes the human being's attempts to preserve his identity and to make his place in the world. Schools, therefore, must address themselves to the development of the general creative abilities in students, which David Ausubel describes as "a constellation of problem solving and personality traits that, like general intelligence, not only facilitate discovery learning, but also help implement the expression of substantive creativity."[11]

The Creative Process

It is generally accepted that a child grows into a whole personality by having his developmental needs satisfied. These basic growth needs are physical, mental, social, emotional, and spiritual. Every child possesses the basic need to know why, to ask why, to learn, and to seek knowledge of all kinds. These needs lead him to a strong sense of intellectual security once he arrives at a realization of what he knows. This is the cognitive side of creativity; but the other side is an emotional one, and it is this aspect which provides the individual with his distinction and sensitivity. Perhaps because the emotional needs of a child are not so easily identified, parents and educators have paid less attention to their development; yet to ignore such development is to invite a kind of far-reaching paralysis which may well cripple the individual in his attempts to find a meaningful existence. Clark Moustakas makes this problem quite clear.

> In a climate where freedom and choice are denied, the individual comes to reject his own senses. He does not make full use of his perceptions and faculties in determining which experiences contribute to self-realization and which are irrelevant or impeding; he no longer uses his own organs and powers to create reality and to venture into new life. Since the individual does not trust his own immediate experience, and the response of his senses to lead him to new experience, he is neither open to himself nor to the world.[12]

Such conditions do not have to exist; the urge to create seems to be present at least to some degree in everyone. Often, though, as we get older, the impulse becomes hidden behind a facade of indifference which results in a kind of uniformity of behavior. According to E. Paul Torrance, the repression of the creative impulse may lead to serious learning disabilities and heavy reliance upon authoritarian structures.[13] Hence it is important to recognize that everyone does have the potential for some form of creative expression and, more important, that manifestations of such potential can be increased or decreased by the way children are treated while they are growing up.

Although some confusion about the term "creativity" exists, research recognizes some general attributes of creativity that help distinguish the degree of creativeness within an individual.[14] It is commonly accepted, for instance, that the truly creative person is sensitive to problem situations and to his surroundings, for no work of a creative nature is possible unless it is based on sensitive experience, sensitivity coming from an ability to see defects, needs, and deficiencies or the ability to see the odd and the unusual.[15]

Sensitivity, in turn, leads the creative person to a fluency of ideas. The creative person may possess a high degree of ideational fluency, which in ordinary terms is simply an indication of the number of ideas that a person may have when thinking about one item. [16] The creative individual also may have a high rate of associational fluency; on a verbal level this would mean a rapid production of words meeting specific requirements. This ability is extremely useful in advertising, where new slogans or specific word images are needed. In fact, business is rapidly recognizing the value of individuals who have both kinds of fluency, and frequently these people are used in brainstorming sessions to give spark to ideas and products. [17]

Flexibility is another characteristic often associated with the creative person. The creative person adjusts quickly to new situations and new forms; but not only must the creator continually adapt his expression to the medium which he uses, but he must also take continuous advantage of the changes in his ideas and responses which he obtained during the creative process. Naturally such elasticity involves a high degree of originality that will show itself in the uncommonness of the verbal or sensory responses.

Closely allied to the principle of flexibility is the ability to rearrange and redefine. To take an object and shift its function or to start with the whole and arrive at details enables the creator to penetrate the nature of his experience. From this penetration will come examples of synthesis and closure, or the ability to relate various materials to each other in meaningful ways. Ultimately we find that creative actions take on a coherence of organization; there is a kind of economy which becomes a part of the esthetic sense; and the ability to express the utmost with the least means and effort frequently characterizes the creative endeavor.

Despite the recognition of many characteristic behaviors, however, the actual process of creation remains a mysterious one. Study of the creative process is hampered by the fact that, being a process, it is in motion. If one could stop it for observation, what would he see? The only way to learn about the creative process is to attempt to "gain insight into the underlying, nonrational associative concepts which flow under the articulated surface phenomena." [18]

William Shutz in his work *Joy,* which explores the freeing of the individual for the purpose of better recognizing his own potentials, suggests that the creative process involves several stages, each stage continuing what has preceded it and merging into other experiences until the final entity is realized. The opening stage is the freeing of the individual; a person must open himself to past, present, and future experiences and be able to perceive and sense his environment. John Wilson and Mildred C. Robeck have found in their studies of young people that a person does not create out of nothing.

What he uses are the mental, aesthetic or emotional materials available to him from previous experiences. When these experiences have been restricted, cabined or confined as is the case with many disadvantaged children they have only meager resources to call upon. [19]

This first stage begins, then, when an individual has a need strong enough to touch off activity. The period of time involved may be quite short, or it may stretch over a period of years, depending upon the nature of the problem and the various knowledge, habits, and skills which the individual brings to bear upon the problem.

The first stage is followed by one of association—a drawing together of experiences into some kind of meaningful relationship. The time period involved here is sometimes referred to as one of incubation because the activity is often of an unconscious kind. A searching is going on and a gradual ripening of the solution; hence considerable restlessness and frustration occur.

Then come the stages of expression and evaluation. Elements which have been connected must now be emitted in some way—through spoken or written language or through bodily movement. Once the expression has occurred, evaluation takes place. As human beings we tend to generate many products, but we have to evaluate to determine the worth of these products. Thus during this stage the creator painstakingly checks, tests, criticizes, elaborates, and polishes until he is satisfied with the worth of the final product.

And finally we have the important ingredient of perseverance, which can be found in all stages of creation. Without it, most creative endeavor would not occur, because the creative process involves constantly trying out new roles, new expressions, and new knowledge, meeting with both success and failure. [20] E. Paul Torrance summarizes the creative learning process in this way:

> Learning creatively takes place in the process of becoming sensitive to or aware of problems, deficiencies, gaps in knowledge, missing elements, disharmonies and so on; bringing together in new relationships available existing information; defining the difficulty of identifying the missing elements; searching for solutions, making guesses or formulating hypotheses about the problems or deficiencies; testing and retesting them; perfecting them, and finally communicating the results. [21]

These abilities to create and to express set mankind apart from other living creatures. Since creativity is one of mankind's inherent powers, a person must be free to develop his mind, his body, and his imaginative faculties in order to realize himself fully as an individual. At one extreme the creative process may be nothing more than engaging in elementary problem-solving activity; at the other extreme it may invite a high degree of originality. The process is, however, always more than mere intellectual gymnastics. Mary Lee Marksberry points out, "It [the creative process] is an absorption of the total person in the problem; and it becomes an aesthetic experience which is satisfying to the creator both for the actions which define and compose it and for the final product." 22

Creativity in the Schools

Our present educational system has tended to overlook this fundamental process. Our schools emphasize the need to learn factual information. To a great extent the passing or failing of courses is predicated on the ability to master or memorize certain bits of information that are already known to the instructors. On the whole, our present educational process is too exclusively verbal and cognitive. That such conditions exist should not be surprising, however, for in an age which calls for accountability, profit margins, and less spending, educators feel they have little choice but to concentrate on those aspects of education which can be most easily used to pacify public demands. The result is a program of instruction heavily weighted in favor of the mastery of easily measured cognitive tasks. To achieve an adequately balanced, diversified program in general education which will move to meet the various needs of all students, more emphasis will have to be placed on the esthetic and creative aspects of learning. Efforts to develop students' powers of sense perception, imagination, empathy, and bodily control are desperately needed. The ability to learn differs from age to age and from individual to individual, but we must realize that this ability to learn involves not only intellectual capacity but also social, perceptual, physical, and psychological factors.

But creative expression has rarely been recognized as a serious objective of education. Instead, creative behavior is often interpreted as being aggressive or hostile; as a matter of fact, it can become just that if ideas and questions are continually rejected. Findings of research suggest that educators frequently are too quick to reward docility and "niceness" in students and that the independent, offbeat, and sometimes unruly students whom we frequently undervalue and deplore often may have the greatest potential for creative achievement. That the latter students will get the opportunities to recognize and use their potential seems somewhat unlikely. E. Paul Torrance, who has done extensive studies on creativity and creative behavior, uncovered some rather dismaying evidence in this respect. In 1959-60 he conducted a study in Minnesota to determine what kinds of objectives in learning were most important to educators. He asked Minnesota social science teachers to list the three most important objectives in one of their courses; taking the results, he discovered that the objectives fell into the following categories:

Cognitive objectives (those which called for recognizing, realizing, becoming aware of, or becoming acquainted with various kinds of information): 70.9 percent.

Memory objectives (those which called for remembering, acquiring distinct or thorough knowledge of, or learning thoroughly information): 5.3 percent.

Convergent objectives (those which called for behavioral norms, right attitudes, right solutions): 18.7 percent.

Divergent objectives (those which called for independent thinking, constructive action, creative expression, liberal and inquiring action): 1.7 percent.

Evaluative objectives (those which called for critical thinking, assessing, selecting and comparing, judging, deciding): 3.6 percent. [23]

Most authorities would agree that creative activity usually accompanies those areas which are covered by the divergent and evaluative objectives. Although the study sample was small, this study suggests that the emphasis in teaching may not fall on those approaches which allow for and encourage creative endeavor; instead there is a definite hint that students are steered toward uniformity in behavior.

Perhaps one of the most powerful ways in which a culture encourages or discourages creative behavior is the way by which teachers and parents encourage or discourage, punish or reward certain personality characteristics as they develop in children. To test this idea, Torrance and his associates selected over fifty empirical studies which differentiated highly creative people from those less creative. Using the information gathered in these studies, Torrance developed a checklist whose purpose was to determine the characteristics of the ideal child as viewed by parents and teachers. His study sample was drawn from twelve states in America and nine countries outside the United States. Initial results showed that in the United States the characteristics most favored by educators and parents (given in order of preference) were the following: (1) independence of thinking, (2) curiosity, (3) sense of humor, (4) consideration of others, (5) industriousness, (6) receptiveness to others' ideas, (7) determination, (8) self-starting, (9) sincerity, (10) thoroughness.[24] Such behaviors as asking questions, preferring complex tasks, willingness to take risks, and independence in judgment were all regarded as much less desirable by those participating in the study.

But the inequality of treatment goes even further. We need only look at the Creative Art Scale that is sometimes used to determine signs of creativity by those involved in a study of the creative process. Points on this scale may be earned by accomplishing any of the following:

1. Having poems, stories or articles published in a magazine
2. Winning an art competition award

3. Composing music which is given in public performance
4. Playing major roles in plays
5. Winning speech contests. [25]

One cannot argue that the performances indicated above are not manifestations of creative endeavor. But the focus is on public display, and the truly creative child may be quite inhibited by such an emphasis on public approval. In fact, creative activity, which is a very personal thing, is frequently inhibited by a conglomeration of experiences; even television and radio may be considered inhibiting, for they often infringe on what little time is left for children to put fleeting thoughts into action or words.

Still another aspect of the confusion surrounding creative behavior, and perhaps illustrated in the scale above, is the relationship between the terms "creative" and "talented." According to George I. Thomas and Joseph Crescimbeni, the talented individual must demonstrate that he is more than creative; that is, he must show outstanding ability in his field and that, if given advanced level instruction, he could probably be successful in that field as an occupation. [26] This kind of distinction seems to be a valid one and should be remembered when we are discussing creative expression and the creative individual, for we are not necessarily talking about polished or public displays of abilities.

Intelligence is another factor which enters the discussion of creativity. People often assume that high intelligence is essential for creative expression, but this is not always true. Actually, if we were to attempt to identify signs of creativity in children merely on the basis of intelligence tests—a practice which is, unfortunately, quite widespread—we would eliminate from consideration nearly 70 percent of the most creative. The reason for this is that traditional tests of intelligence are filled with tasks which require memory and convergent thinking—two characteristics which are not particularly valid indicators of creativity. [27]

To their credit, though, educators and psychologists have recognized the need for students to have experiences in early childhood that strengthen sensibilities and encourage strong expression. They have come to recognize that when children are permitted to think their way through to new understandings, the concepts they derive in the process have greater depth, understanding, and durability. What must be remembered, too, is that in authentic experience the subject matter is related to the learner. It arouses and sustains his interest. It is not something to be memorized and repeated, but rather it is raw material to be shaped and developed. Most adults have noted at one time or another that in almost every child at the age of five or six, artistic and esthetic interests are active, alert, sensitive, and eager. But soon after that age—about the time children enter formal schooling—a change begins to appear. Ruth Sawyer, who as a well-known teller of children's stories has ample opportunity to observe children at different stages of development, agrees that the promising early signs of interest do not last very long.

> ... midway in childhood something begins to happen. The cord is cut. There must be an adjustment to a factual, material world. Children begin to conform. Adults help the process along that adjustment may be as swift and as resistless as possible. Children's minds are railroaded from this station to that, all plainly marked on the map called Education. That space so boundless in babyhood, that heavenly pasture for play and joy unbounded becomes narrowed down with each year, each grade, until it becomes no wider than your thumb. [28]

How does it happen? Society emphasizes specialization, and so education, which is especially vulnerable to social pressures, tends to ignore the exploratory values of education for all children and concentrates instead on specific tasks and skills. It may be easy for a student in the lower grades to reveal how he feels about things and people; but as he gets older, his sensitivity to what others think can hold him back unless he has had many experiences which have given him confidence that he can say or do things which people may accept or reject. As Charles Silberman points out in *Crisis in the Classroom,* schools discourage students from developing the capacity to learn by and for themselves. They make it impossible for a youngster to take responsibility for his own education, for the schools are structured in such a manner as to make students totally dependent upon teachers. [29] The effects of this gradual but insidious erosion of creative expression can be seen today even in college students, who suffer both emotionally and academically because of their uncertainty regarding what they are capable of doing and who they really are. Richard Lewis summarizes the problem this way:

> ... eventually the initial concept of myth, of fantasy, of nonsense, of intuitive thinking that all children possess becomes, in part, a very threatening aspect to the educational establishment. . . . Educators see a lack of learning situations within it; in other words, it can't be measured, because it is the most immeasurable of all things.[30]

And so, in an age which places such high premiums on accountability and scientific explanation, the creative process and its accompanying behaviors are ignored. The educational program is not equipped at the present time to deal with the variations and the idiosyncrasies which so often are a part of creative behavior. Consequently, some type of normative behavior is instilled so that the "business of learning" can proceed with a minimum of interruption. The present educational system is basically coercive in a negative sense, and the establishment of standard behavior norms is a very important part of the educational framework. Because this approach is so pervasive, few teachers or administrators escape playing a role in the coercion.

Developing Creative Individuals

Ideally, however, all children should have an educational environment where they can work with many kinds of media, where they can explore new fields of study, and where they can experience both success and failure as they work within challenging and yet supportive situations. Certainly a child needs skills to meet the realities of life; but along with the skills he needs imagination and a philosophy that can guide his growth. The child who is allowed gradually to fulfill his creative capacities along with the other basic aspects of his personality feels freer and more confident in meeting the environmental forces of daily living. Free-thinking and creative men and women do not develop in situations which discourage inquiry and stress passive acceptance: rather they develop in an open and active environment that encourages the development of creative response.

Stimulating creative expression does not present the monumental challenge which people have suggested. Hughes Mearns points out:

> Children seem to be driven by an inner necessity of putting forth something; that it should turn out to be beautiful is not their concern; their impulse at its best is to place something in the outside world that is already (or almost ready) in their inside world of perceiving, thinking, feeling; they measure their success or failure by the final resemblance of the thing done to the thing imagined. [31]

Thus it is that the value of a discovery in the mental life of a person is the contribution it makes to the creatively active mind. It is not so important that no one has thought of the same idea before. If the product is sincere, fresh and new and original in quality, even if others make the same discovery, the real importance is that it is first-hand, not taken second-hand from some other source. [32]

The fostering of creative expression in learning, then, jogs students out of passive acceptances and mechanical routines; it makes familiar things different and worthy of noticing, provides new devices for thought, and encourages experimentation. As its central purpose, the creative approach to education should always be directed toward making students alert, curious, responsive, independent individuals. In a world bombarded with crisis after crisis, decision after decision, society needs adults who can feel free to think and act for themselves.

In a study of kindergarten children, Torrance and Fortson compared the effects of creative teaching practices with a traditional instructional approach. They found that children exposed to teaching in which activities were planned to elicit maximum amounts of creative thinking—by encouraging students to offer ideas freely, hazard guesses, and predict outcomes—differed significantly on a number of measures of creative thinking from children who had experienced traditional instruction. Of particular significance was the discovery that the reported differences in creative thinking were found after only one semester's exposure to a creative teaching program. [33]

The principal way, then, to develop such people is to provide ample practice in the classroom where the climate is emotionally appropriate and supportive rather than punishing. Provide each child with the freedom to learn by himself with supporting guidance from the teacher, if necessary, and the result will undoubtedly be an adult who can think and create for himself. If we ignore this function, "the individual ceases to be himself; he adopts entirely the kind of personality offered to him by cultural patterns; and he therefore becomes exactly as all others are and as they expect him to be." [34]

The individual grows by assimilating, reorganizing, and using selected elements from the culture in which he lives. Recent experiments and research have shown that all people, even mental retardates, can experience creative expression. Contrary to popular belief, what a person knows or does not know may have no bearing on the creative action in which he may participate. [35] It follows, then, that the greater the opportunities to increase sensitivities, the greater will be the opportunity for rich learning. If a child is to become a free individual, free from both internal and external fears, he should be encouraged to use his imagination day after day. This emphasis upon the imaginative response will help to lead him into making constructive responses to varying situations. A child has the right to know that all feelings are natural, but he also needs to learn to channel his feelings in ways that are acceptable to himself and to others. He needs to work off some of his feelings—to give strong expression to strong impressions—in constructive fashion rather than keeping them bottled within himself. The child is, after all, a genuine primitive, and as such needs little or no instruction for expression; but he does need materials, and his surroundings must be those which will call forth efforts of worthwhile endeavor.

Students look to the school for opportunities to express their creativity—rightly so, for Americans are fond of saying that education in a democracy should help individuals develop fully their potential. Schools are anxious that the children they educate grow into fully functioning persons. But we cannot say that someone is fully functioning mentally if the abilities involved in creative expression remain undeveloped or paralyzed. How do we determine whether such paralysis exists? One way is to observe student behavior and answer questions such as the following:

1. What kinds of thinking do students display?
2. How resourceful are they?
3. Are they becoming more responsible?
4. Are they learning to give thoughtful explanations of the things they do and see?
5. Do they believe their own ideas to be of value?
6. Can they share ideas and opinions with others?
7. Do they relate similar experiences? [36]

These questions suggest some other considerations. Certainly if creative programs are to emerge in teaching, much will have to change. Since creative expression is an uncertain and often disturbing activity, it can only be developed in a school with courageous and liberal-minded approval of its value and worth. Administrative leadership at all levels will need to create an environment in which "freedom to learn" is a dominant and real characteristic for both teachers and students and not just another empty educational slogan. But to establish creative expression as a central aspect of the educational process will not be an easy task. If an attitude prevails that we are already meeting the creative needs of all children and thus no changes need to be made, we can hardly expect any sudden amount of creative experimentation on the part of either students or teachers.

Part of the reason for the present attitude toward creativity in education can be traced to a basic work/play dichotomy in our culture. A child is supposed to enjoy play, but it is considered peculiar if he likes work. For years, learning has been associated only with the glum, and we even go so far as to refer respectfully to the "serious" student. Still, there is no reason why learning should not be so enjoyable and meaningful to the individual as play; after all, the little child of five or six finds learning a joyful experience. As Eric Hoffer suggests in his essay "The Playful Mood," men never philosophize or think more freely than when they know that their speculation or tinkering leads to no weighty results. Inventions such as the telescope and microscope were initially conceived as toys. Hoffer also makes the observation that "the chances are that the momentous discoveries and inventions of the Neolithic Age which made possible the rise of civilization and which formed the basis of everyday life until yesterday were made by childlike, playful people." [37]

This is not to suggest that all education should simply become a recreational free-for-all. To those who fear that creativity in education is simply a cover for a new form of "soft" education, there is the reassurance that the bases of various disciplines remain as vital sources of probing, meaningful questions leading to evaluation of alternatives in possible courses of behavior. To those who advocate a return to the "good old days," to the "fundamentals," and to the often repressive atmosphere, we can only point to the present products of our system and to the problems in our culture. Once such methods may have been adequate; but today we cannot stand on yesterday, for tomorrow is already here.

But why must the schools bear almost alone the responsiblity for developing creative expression?

> It is a matter of the greatest urgency that our educational institutions realize that . . . the classroom is now in a vital struggle for survival with the immensely persuasive "outside" world created by new informational media. Education must shift from instruction, from imposing of stencils, to discovery—to probing and exploration. . . .[38]

In several ways the school is the most effective agent we have for meeting the creative needs of a large population. The schools come into contact with more people at their most impressionable stages of development than any other agency. And then, too, teachers can be trained to foster creative expression and to provide the necessary skills and opportunities for creative learning. The school is also best equipped to provide sequential experiences necessary for the growth of intellectual skills, knowledge, and attitudes.

Most important, however, are the conditions under which the creative process will be nurtured. McLuhan is quite right when he says, "The young today live mythically and in depth. But they encounter instruction in situations organized by means of classified information—subjects are unrelated, they are visually conceived in terms of a blueprint. Many of our institutions suppress all the natural direct experiences of youth. . . ."[39] J. D. Ferebee suggests that to establish a responsive learning environment conducive to the stimulation of the creative process, the following principles should be considered:

1. Build an atmosphere for receptive listening
2. Fend off negative criticism
3. Make children aware of what is good
4. Stir the sluggish and deepen the shallow
5. Make sure that every sincere effort, however poorly executed, brings enough satisfaction to the child to enable him to want to try again
6. Heighten sensory awareness
7. Keep alive the zest in creative activity
8. Be wise enough to halt the activity temporarily when creativity runs thin.[40]

All areas of the curriculum will be considered instruments to develop creative learning, providing, among other things, open-ended problem situations and more democratic procedures within the learning process.

It will be necessary to de-emphasize formal evaluation of learning because the psychological processes associated with creative thinking require, for their maximum operation, a context free from, or minimally influenced by, anxiety that arises from fear of academic evaluation or consequence of error.[41] This does not mean that all evaluation will cease. The nature of the creative process actually invites continuous evaluation, but within the context of the creation, not as an external and punitive element as has been so frequently the case in the past. As a consequence, teachers will have to be more willing to accept hypotheses and conjecture, recognizing that these are only a part of the testing and trying-on of roles and situations. There must be as well an accompanying demand for a more student-oriented philosophy of learning, as opposed to the teacher-goal oriented philosophy which has characterized so much of the educational venture up to this time.

The challenge to education is to build the foundations for a school in which the uniqueness of the individual may truly develop and to provide the necessary opportunities for him to search for his identity and a meaningful relationship with the world. It will not be an easy task; but it is a necessary one, and the ultimate rewards will justify the labor. As Carl Rogers says in *Freedom to Learn:*

> When I realize the incredible potential in the ordinary student, I want to try to release it. We are working hard to release the incredible energy in the atom and the nucleus of the atom. If we do not devote equal energy—yes, and equal money—to the release of the potential of the individual person then the enormous discrepancy between our level of physical energy resources and human energy resources will doom us to a deserved and universal destruction.[42]

Notes

1. Sheridan, "Creative Language Experiences in High School," p. 563.
2. Calabria, "The Why of Creative Dramatics," p. 182.
3. Scofield, "A Creative Climate," p. 5.
4. I. A. Taylor, "The Nature of Creative Process," pp. 51-82, passim.
5. Coggin, *Uses of Drama,* p. 228.
6. Durland, *Creative Dramatics for Children,* p. 27.
7. Schactel, *Metamorphosis: On the Development of Affect, Perception, Attention, and Memory,* p. 243.
8. Lowenfeld and Brittain, *Creative and Mental Growth,* 4th ed., p. 2.
9. Rubin, "Creativity in the Curriculum," p. 75.
10. Holbrook, "Creativity in the English Programme," p. 10.
11. Ausubel, "Creativity, General Creative Abilities, and the Creative Individual," p. 345.
12. Moustakas, "Creativity and Conformity in Education," p. 174.
13. Torrance, *Guiding Creative Talent,* p. 128.
14. Lowenfeld, "Current Research on Creativity," pp. 538-40.

15. Ausubel, "Creativity, General Creative Abilities, and the Creative Individual," p. 345.
16. A test often administered to children to determine their rate of ideational fluency is to give them an object such as a brick and have them list as rapidly as possible all the various ideas they have for the use of the brick. See Torrance, *Rewarding Creative Behavior*, pp. 298-300, for other tests and explanations of ideational and associational fluency.
17. See Gordon, *Synectics*, for an explanation of how these particular aspects of creativity are developed and used. See also Clark, *Brainstorming*, and Rapp, "The Brainstorming Attitude."
18. Gordon, *Synectics*, p. 3.
19. Wilson and Robeck, "Creativity in the Very Young," p. 63.
20. Shutz, *Joy*, p. 55. See the following for additional discussion of the creative process: Hutchinson, *How to Think Creatively*; Jones, "The Creativity Problem"; Murphy, "The Process of Creative Thinking"; Patrick, "What Is Creative Thinking?"; Piers, et al., "The Identification of Creativity in Adolescents."
21. Torrance, *Encouraging Creativity in the Classroom*, p. 1.
22. Marksberry, *Foundation of Creativity*, p. 20.
23. Torrance, *Guiding Creative Talent*, p. 29. © 1962, Prentice-Hall, Inc., Englewood Cliffs, N.J. Reprinted with permission.
24. Torrance, *Rewarding Creative Behavior*, p. 228; see pp. 221-34 for a complete analysis of the study. See also Torrance, *Encouraging Creativity in the Classroom*, pp. 16-20.
25. Barron, "Creativity: What Research Says about It," p. 19.
26. Thomas and Crescimbeni, *Individualizing Instruction in the Elementary School*, p. 161.
27. Torrance, *Guiding Creative Talent*, p. 4.
28. Sawyer, *The Way of the Storyteller*, p. 81.
29. Silberman, *Crisis in the Classroom*, p. 135.
30. Lewis, "Do Children Have a Culture of Their Own?" p. 71.
31. Mearns, "The Creative Spirit and Its Significance for Education," p. 17.
32. Dewey, *Construction and Criticism*, unpaged.
33. Torrance and Fortson, "Creativity among Young Children and the Creative-Aesthetic Approach," pp. 27-30.
34. Fromm, *Escape from Freedom*, p. 185.
35. Lowenfeld and Brittain, *Creative and Mental Growth*, 4th ed., p. 41.
36. Torrance, *Guiding Creative Talent*, p. 6. © 1962, Prentice-Hall, Inc., Englewood Cliffs, N.J. Reprinted with permission
37. Hoffer, *The Ordeal of Change*, p. 91.
38. McLuhan and Fiore, *The Medium Is the Massage*, p. 100.
39. Ibid.
40. Ferebee, "Learning Form through Creative Expression," p. 78.
41. Cohen, "Creativity: An Implicit Goal in Education," p. 176.
42. Rogers, *Freedom to Learn*, p. 125.

*It is comparatively easy to develop drama, but more
difficult to develop people; it is equally simple to assess
and measure some aspects of the development of drama
itself, but to do so can negate the primary intention of
developing people through drama.*

Brian Way, *Development through Drama*, p. 2.

2 The Historical Development of Children's Drama

Around the turn of the century a renaissance in educational
philosophy introduced significant changes in childhood education. The
emerging principles and procedures placed much more emphasis upon
children's growth and development in the experience of learning. In
particular, educators came to recognize that the best possible preparation for creativity in life lay in providing opportunities for children to
create constantly out of their present knowledge.

Authorities in what came to be called the "progressive" movement
suggested that there were three assumptions underlying the emerging
educational approach. These concepts were that (1) proficiency and
learning come not only from reading and listening but from action,
from doing, and from experience; (2) good work is more often the
result of spontaneous effort and free interest than it is of compulsion
and forced application; (3) the natural means of study in youth is
play.[1]

As will be shown later, many educators of the late 1800s and early
1900s accepted these concepts and searched for ways to involve the
student more fully in his learning, stressing the active as opposed to the
passive in educational experiences. The effectiveness with which
creative arts experiences could contribute to the growth and personality
development of the child began to attract interest. Capitalizing also on
the idea that every human being has, at some time, the impulse to play,
teachers looked for ways to incorporate play activity into the learning
process, not fully realizing at first that play is often a learning
experience in itself. Gradually more attention was paid to the way
children learn and to the activities in which they spend much of their

time. As a result, educators discovered a strong dramatic impulse which seemed to run through many of the normal activities of children. The presence of such an impulse was not surprising. Since the early beginnings of civilization, song, dance, speech, and ritual have been used to dramatize important occasions, new knowledge, and customs, as a means of drawing groups of individuals together in a common bond of socialized feeling as well as for direct communication.[2] Noting the effectiveness with which children seemed to communicate with each other by dramatic means, school authorities began to consider making room for dramatic activity in their programs.

Such activities, however, did not spread immediately into the various curricula of the late 1800s. The first evidence that American education was beginning to move toward creative drama came from some of the educational innovations which Edward Austin Sheldon introduced in about 1853 to the public schools of Oswego, New York. Sheldon, a superintendent of schools, had spent time traveling and gathering information about educational practices, particularly those in Europe. One of the educational philosophies which attracted his attention was that of Johann Heinrich Pestalozzi (1746-1827). Pestalozzi, a Swiss educator, had rebelled against the eighteenth century European teaching practices which often tended to be unrealistic in the way they prepared students for regular life. To Pestalozzi the "ultimate aim of education is not perfection in the accomplishments of the school, but a fitness for life; not the acquirement of habits of blind obedience, and of prescribed diligence, but a preparation for independent action."[3] To realize his aim, Pestalozzi placed a great deal of emphasis upon exercises in sense impressions and oral language use. Through these exercises he hoped to encourage students to react to their environment and become more aware of their actions.

Many of these exercises became known as "object lessons" and were direct attempts to get students to observe and discuss. Such teaching represented definite attempts to make use of concrete instructional materials found in a child's physical environment as well as specific experiences drawn from his social environment. Hence a student would often be handed an object and invited to identify its qualities and uses by means of various sensory tests. The activity was part of the overall plan to have the child prepare for life by actually instructing himself through reasoning, under the guidance of the teacher. The principal fault with this kind of instruction was that the child frequently failed to go beyond the mere identification of the objects; he failed to capitalize upon the sensory impressions and use them for other creative endeavors and comparisons.

Margaret Jones of the Home and Colonial Society in London, England, summarized the basic Pestalozzian theories as follows:

1. The teacher must begin instruction with the senses.
2. A student should never be told what he can discover for himself.
3. The child should not be trained to merely listen; he should be actively involved in learning, since activity is a law of childhood.
4. There should be an abundant variety of activities available to the student.
5. Faculties should be cultivated in their natural order, first forming the mind and then furnishing it.
6. Reduce every subject to its basic elements and present one difficulty at a time.
7. Instruct step by step, since the measure of information is not what the teacher can give, but what the child can receive.
8. Every lesson should have a definite purpose.
9. Develop the idea first and then offer the term so language skills can be developed.
10. Proceed from the simple to the difficult, from the known to the unknown, the particular to the general, the concrete to the abstract.
11. Use the process of synthesis before analysis [*sic*].[4]

Many of these principles still can be found in today's educational philosophies. Sheldon's admiration for Pestalozzi's work caused him to introduce many of Pestalozzi's teaching theories into American schools. Sheldon's early reforms did much to help free the classroom environment from its formal rigidity, its almost total reliance upon rote methods of learning, and its emphasis on almost exclusively written communication. These characteristics were replaced by the idea of spontaneous activity and the value of oral discussion in the teaching-learning process. Fostered, too, was more concern for the individual's creativity. Because of his attempts at reform, Sheldon soon became well known throughout the United States, and his schools were visited by educators from all over the country.

By the 1870s the Pestalozzian methods were beginning to influence much of the educational instruction in America. In 1874 Sheldon published his *Manual of Elementary Instruction,* which included a number of illustrations suggesting how dramatic activities could be worked into the classroom. For example, in one lesson, which used a nineteenth century painting entitled "The Blind Girl," the teacher was advised to help children exercise their perception by letting them describe the picture. In particular, how did the girls differ in appearance? How did the children know one of the girls in the picture was blind and was being led by the other? Once this exercise in perception was completed, Sheldon suggested that the teacher involve the students in an exercise of conception, calling on them to perform while simulating blindness. This, in turn, would be followed by having students think of and enact situations in which they could help blind individuals—going up stairs, opening doors, crossing streets.[5]

Sheldon's influence was strong, and other educators began to make suggestions of their own. Francis Wayland Parker directed the activities of the Cook County Normal School in Chicago, Illinois, from 1883 to 1896 and made that institution famous for its excellent training programs. Parker emphasized in his many talks with teachers that it was useless to force students to think of concepts that were not in their minds. He recognized the significance of a child's learning through reverbalization—a process whereby students use their own words in learning, not just the teacher's.[6]

Along with Sheldon and Pestalozzi, Parker was opposed to heavy reliance on textbooks, believing that they often created unnecessary barriers between students and teachers. Thus he emphasized the wisdom of educating through the child's desire for activity.

> All education is by self-activity, and, at the same time it may be said that self-activity is an evidence of human growth beyond the threshold of the educative stage; that the basis of human development, that is, heredity, the physical organism of the body, and the spontaneous action of external attributes form the foundation or present the conditions absolutely necessary for self-activity.[7]

Parker also felt strongly about the importance of myth and fantasy to children, believing that the presence of myth and fantasy in children's lives had a direct relationship to the development of creative power in a child. His advice to teachers about how to use this presence included the following:

> You know very well how eager a child is for stories that arouse its love for rhythm and excite its fancy. The child most delights in fairy tales, the mythical treasures of the ages. The cruel bonds of stern reality are broken, and it enters a beautiful and invisible world, peopled by creations of its own fancy. If a child were limited in its early stages to the world of reality, if it could not go out into the unknown world, the invisible world, it would lead the life of a brute.[8]

Parker's views about education, particularly those regarding the process of reverbalization, had considerable impact upon teaching methods of the time, and the reverbalization process is still a major aspect of the teaching technique in creative dramatic activity.

The Francis W. Parker School, founded in 1901 in Chicago a year before Parker's death, carried on his philosophy and became committed to the idea of developing expressiveness in its students by training them in the various arts. Chief among these arts was dramatization. The school's founders offered a number of justifications for the attention paid to drama in the curriculum, but three of these reasons are particularly interesting since they appear again in later definitions of children's drama. According to faculty members of the Parker School, the purposes of drama were (1) to afford the dramatic instinct in students an opportunity for expression; (2) to train and develop the student in terms of imagination, breadth of sympathy, and understanding of human nature, as well as to show him how to subordinate the self to the whole and to develop and control the emotions; and finally (3) to give opportunities to shy and reserved children to express themselves under the cover of a different personality, and to develop individuals possessed of unusual native ability.[9]

During the 1920s, another educator, William Wirt of the Gary, Indiana, schools, popularized the approach known as the platoon system of work-study-play. One major purpose of this plan was to utilize all aspects of the school plant and curriculum as fully as possible. The proponents of the platoon system insisted that all educational activity be synthesized; occasionally this directive caused some difficulty, such as during the time allotted for auditorium activity.

Students were assigned to an auditorium each day for a certain period of time. While there they participated in a variety of activities designed to involve all students and to have direct correlation with activities going on in other parts of the school's program. The auditorium activities were usually under the supervision of trained speech and drama teachers, who soon found that dramatics was one of the easiest and most effective ways to involve the majority of children and at the same time meet the educational objectives of the curriculum. The way this was accomplished was described by a teacher in a platoon school.

> Our dramatization is worked out in the home room and finished in the auditorium. Again, poems, and jingles, character study, lessons in morals and manners, oral and written book reviews, plays, games, expeditions, reading and exchange of letters, story-telling, picture study, keeping shop, store, banks, receptions, teas are used. There is no end to the work that can be unloaded on the auditorium teacher, but to get results the other teachers must be on the job, too, in all the different departments.[10]

This kind of approach became so popular that special courses such as the following eventually were introduced into the training of prospective teachers.

B-61 Auditorium Activities

A practical course covering all speech activities of children, primary, elementary, junior high, and senior high schools, as they may function in the auditorium or assembly period. The auditorium period as a speech laboratory using every form of speech activity and all types of literature—story, dramatization, play, poem. The auditorium period as a correlating, integrating center with samples of classroom programs. Emphasis on materials and methods. Demonstrations. Observations optional.[11]

Sheldon, Parker, and Wirt had considerable influence upon the direction of education in the United States; all three were involved in the training of teachers, with Sheldon, especially, doing a great deal in this area.[12] With these men leading the way, the ideas of freer school environments and greater utilization of dramatic and creative activity became quite firmly implanted in the curricula of some schools during this period.

But it was not until Winifred Ward began working in the 1920s and 1930s with the public schools of Evanston, Illinois, that the idea of children's drama and its role in education really began to develop. Ward had been teaching at Northwestern University when she became intrigued by the apparent connections between dramatic play and learning. Hoping that she might explore these connections more closely, she started in 1923 to work with elementary students in the Evanston school system.[13] At first beginning with just one class, she soon found herself teaching a number of grades, and eventually she was put in charge of dramatic activities for the system; this resulted in her training a number of other teachers to work with her. Ward's work met with such success and enthusiasm that she incorporated her findings into a course for teachers. It was from this early work in the schools and with teachers that Winifred Ward's theories about the uses of creative dramatics grew.

In 1930, the publication of Ward's first book, *Creative Dramatics for the Upper Grades and Junior High School,*[14] generated considerable nationwide interest among educators. Children's theater directors and elementary teachers in particular began requesting more information. The term "creative dramatics" had not appeared in earlier writings about dramatic play, and it is thought that Ward was responsible for bringing the term into prominence, starting unofficially in 1925 and appearing officially in 1928 as the title of one of her courses at Northwestern University.[15]

Ward continued her work in the Evanston schools and also served as consultant to many other school districts throughout the United States. Her first book eventually went out of print, but she followed it with other works—*Theatre for Children* (1939) and *Playmaking with Children* (1947); the latter was an even more complete exploration of the relationships between playmaking and the purposes of modern education. Five of these educational purposes were singled out as being the most significant: (1) schools should give children many opportunities to practice democratic ideas; (2) children should learn through meaningful experiences; (3) all children should be encouraged to think creatively; (4) children should be educated for social living; (5) the whole child should be educated—physically, intellectually, and emotionally.[16] Ward was firm in her conviction that all of these purposes could be and would be achieved through students' participation in creative dramatics.

Children's Theater and Creative Dramatics

The term "creative dramatics," however, aroused considerable confusion. Up to the time Ward began her work, most activity with drama had been of a fairly formal nature, with emphasis placed more on performance than anything else. One of the first books to appear that concerned itself with dramatics in the school was John Merrill's and Martha Fleming's *Playmaking and Plays;*[17] yet this work focused primarily on producing plays in the schools and not so much on drama within the classroom for the participants alone. Eventually, to clarify the terminology, theater people began to refer to the category "children's drama"; within this framework could be found two major divisions: children's theater and creative dramatics.

Often children's theater and creative dramatics have been seen to oppose each other. Actually both spring from the same roots—the need of people to role play in order to measure themselves and their own experiences against those of others, not only to see where they are different, but also to discover how they are alike. In this way people achieve a sense of belonging, especially in those aspects of living which are not communicable by words alone.[18]

Children's theater, however, is essentially a group theater experience in which each child participates vicariously as a member of an audience.[19] The principal emphasis in children's theater is upon the formal production of plays for children; the roles may be acted by either amateurs or professionals, children or adults, or a combination of both. Most children's theater is director oriented, with memorized dialogue, scenery, and costumes playing important parts.[20] These aspects form the principal distinctions between creative dramatics and children's theater. In the formal situation the audience is of primary importance to the actors, while in creative dramatics there is no need for an audience other than the members of the group who are not playing at the moment. Creative drama emphasizes the experience of doing and the concrete action of the present rather than the anticipation of future presentation.

Children's theater, of course, has been in existence throughout the world for some time. Its beginning could well have been the French Theatre de l'Ambigu in Paris, founded in 1769,[21] or it is sometimes claimed that the first true theater for children was created in 1784 by

Stephanie de Genlic, governness to the children of the Duke of Chartres.[22] The first significant children's theater in the United States did not appear until 1903, when the Children's Educational Theatre was founded by Alice Minnie Herts in New York City.[23]

The rather extended time lapse between the establishment of European children's theaters and those in America is easily explained. Europeans took their drama more seriously than did Americans, and as a result many European children's theaters developed permanent professional companies, complete with staff, repertory of plays, and their own auditoriums; frequently, too, such theaters were recipients of state subsidies. These conditions have continued. For instance, in 1966, the Theatre of Friendship in East Berlin had an acting company of forty and a technical staff of fifty-five, along with a repertory of fifteen plays which could be performed in the company's own five-hundred-seat theater; the annual budget was approximately $625,000.[24]

Such theaters led very erratic lives in the United States, frequently finding it difficult to generate sufficient public interest to justify staying open. It first fell to the schools and amateur groups to carry on the tradition of children's theater. Today there is among theater circles an increasing interest in producing dramatic performances directed toward children. Much of this new emphasis can be discovered within college theater departments, Northwestern University and the University of Washington being two pioneers in the field.

Children's theater has received national and international recognition; the American Educational Theatre Association (now the American Theatre Association) created in 1944 a division of their Association called the Children's Theatre Conference.[25] In 1965 the International Association of Theatres for Children and Youth (ASSITEJ) was formed in Paris by representatives from twelve nations: Great Britain, the Soviet Union, France, Belgium, Czechoslovakia, the Netherlands, West Germany, East Germany, Italy, Rumania, Canada, and the United States. The avowed purposes of this organization are (1) to make available information about world children's theater; (2) to promote high artistic standards; (3) to encourage establishment of national centers of children's theater (approximately twenty-two nations have such centers affiliated with the Association); (4) to assist with international tours and translations of plays.[26]

A person may wonder what good children's theater does aside from entertaining children. That purpose, incidentally, is not to be taken lightly, but children do receive additional benefits from attending children's theater productions. Such theater offers the thrill of seeing well-known stories come to life, and students are provided with strong, vicarious experiences through which their emotions can find a welcome release. Each individual can become involved in a play, its characters, plot, and development; and, finally, students come to appreciate the art of theater if the productions are tasteful and well done and if there has been some preliminary preparation for the actual theater experience.[27] As Mabel Wright Henry suggests in an article entitled "The Need for Creative Experiences in Oral Language," children's theater fulfills an important function in the child's educational development.

> [Children's theater] clarifies for him [the child] the ramifications of the story and opens the way for his mind to leap ahead of the players in a stimulating shared experience, where, himself anonymous ... the other world walled out, he focuses on characters caught in situations which require decisions and value judgments. That the child audience responds overtly and without urging indicates the degree of involvement and interaction which seldom comes from contact with the printed page. All this overflows into class discussion, commitment to ideas, and written communication.[28]

Children's theater is an important part of drama for students and provides them with necessary experiences for developing attitudes and knowledge. Creative drama, on the other hand, picks up where children's theater ends. And this division of children's drama is of more immediate importance to the regular classroom teacher and the individual student. We know that the ordinary process of daily living brings with it experiences that we call dramatic. These come in times of crisis, of decision, of giving battle and resolving conflicts. Such experiences are among the roots of our learning and are inseparable parts of us. Much educative activity must recognize the presence of these experiences. Thus, although creative drama remains well grounded in the fundamentals of theater, it aims primarily at the personal development of children, and for this reason has been valuable for education.

Creative dramatics has been defined in numerous ways. Perhaps the clearest definition was offered by Winifred Ward, who defined it as being all forms of improvised drama created by children themselves and played with spontaneous dialogue and action. According to Ward, creative drama has its beginnings in the imaginative play of the young child; as he grows older, however, this dramatic play gradually becomes more structured and evolves into a type of art form. Creative drama can also include creative plays based on ideas and on literature, incidents from the social sciences, original dance-pantomime, creative work in shadow plays and puppetry, and various other integrated projects drawn from many subject fields.[29] Geraldine Brain Siks, a more recent leader in the field of creative dramatics, expanded a bit on Ward's definition. Professor Siks saw creative drama as an art form for children, a group experience in which every child is guided to express himself as he works and plays with others for the joy of creating improvised drama.[30]

Obviously, then, some distinct differences exist between the two forms of children's drama and, as might be expected, considerable controversy has arisen as to which should be given greater emphasis in the curriculum. The advocates of "theater" in education tend to view their work as essentially an "acting to an audience" and the fulfillment of the corresponding responsibilities that such performance entails. They cite reasons, previously discussed, for including children's theater in the regular curriculum.

On the other hand, advocates of creative dramatics feel that for many child actors an audience would be harmful and undesirable, at least until the child recognizes the need for such experience. Those working with creative dramatics also feel that drama as a training for the whole personality is far more important than the development of performance skills. [31] Underlying this point of view is the principle that in the theater of spontaneity the whole community is present. It is in play that children test life without fear; it is in this medium that the strong and the weak work together and discover each other. It is, in the words of Jacob L. Moreno, the place "where reality itself is tested as to its 'reality.' " [32] Adherents of the philosophy that creative dramatics is a means of personality development also stress that drama is a form of play, and play activities are ones in which people expend considerable energy; thus dramatic play allows for utilizing and channeling some of this energy into constructive activity.[33] And still another part of the argument for emphasizing creative drama in education is that drama as an art combines for its purposes all the other arts. Color, form, motion, speech, and music are its media.[34] The process of participating in creative drama, then, encourages students to become more aware and capable of using effectively concentration, imagination, the senses, the voice, the emotions, and the intellect.

And Winifred Ward, again, struck at the basic differences between the advocates of children's theater and those of creative drama. She said:

> Many years of experience with both formal and informal dramatics have convinced me that exhibitional work, whether in music, dance, or creative dramatics, is not conducive to the natural, charming development of any . . . child. No one admires the "show-off" whether he is a child or a grown-up, and the consciousness of being "cute," which comes from the laughter of an adult audience, at first baffles, then stimulates to unwise effort an otherwise delightful child.[35]

Unfortunately, creative dramatics has often been thought of as simply another activity for the classroom. Such a view has proved a pitfall for unwary teachers trying to employ creative drama in their classrooms without being sufficiently familiar with the principles behind it. Too frequently teachers have misunderstood its purposes and have approached creative drama as though it were simply a matter of putting on another play, much in the sense of the usual theatrical performance one sees at the annual Christmas program of the elementary grades or the required assemblies held in many secondary schools throughout the nation. Usually such an approach results in confusion and frustration for both teacher and students. Individuals need to be introduced gradually to the various elements of creative drama and to become comfortable with them before attempting serious applications of the skills to a wide variety of subjects and situations, to say nothing of public performance. As one consultant in elementary education has pointed out, "Creative dramatics . . . is not an isolated subject taught as an independent skill. It is used more than likely . . . to extend and strengthen ideas, knowledge, attitudes and talents of children."[36]

The place for experiences in creative drama is the classroom, not the public stage. In the classroom the personality of the individual student can unfold and blossom in a natural way. From the student's viewpoint, creating plays from stories or experiences with original characterization and dialogue has more meaning than taking part in formal plays for the gratification of parents and teachers.[37] Creative drama emphasizes participation more than product; its chief aim is experience that fosters the child's growth and development in a supportive atmosphere.

Gradually, as more people have become aware of the purposes of children's theater and creative drama, the rift between advocates of children's theater and proponents of creative dramatics has disappeared. People in both areas agree that the two forms of children's drama can exist side by side in the school and, in fact, are directly complementary. Children's theater fulfills certain needs of the child while creative drama takes care of others. For this reason many educators have included both children's theater and creative dramatics in their programs in order to provide the maximum benefits for the young participants. Through the efforts of such people as Winifred Ward, Geraldine Brain Siks, Barbara McIntyre, and others, children's drama has gained in favor in recent years. The benefits to education are still not universally accepted, though, because many people remain unaware of the educational implications of children's drama.

Prior to 1932 no colleges or universities other than Northwestern University were offering curricular work in this field. One of the very first such course offerings for the training of teachers was that of Winifred Ward in 1925; it was described in the following fashion:

Educational Dramatics—Ward

The place of dramatic training in the child's development; fitting of dramatics into the public school curriculum; methods of teaching it. Stories will be dramatized, children's plays directed by members of the class. A large number of plays suitable for primary, intermediate and high school will be read, discussed, and produced.[38]

Eventually, as we have seen, the word began to spread, and by 1957 over two hundred colleges and universities were indicating that they offered some courses in children's drama.[39] But as late as 1963 only approximately two hundred and fifty colleges and universities made such courses available to their students. In 1970 about ten million children a year were seeing live theater performances; in that year 1500 producing units of children's theater existed in the United States; these included professional, college, university, and community theaters, high schools, service organizations, recreation programs, museums, and other groups.[40] But the number of college students preparing to be teachers who have availed themselves of such opportunities remains relatively small.[41] Many teachers still feel unqualified or reluctant to participate in children's drama, particularly in creative dramatics.

Such reluctance is not entirely without justification, since creative dramatics in particular demands considerable time and enormous amounts of patience as well as some dramatic skill. Yet no equipment is necessary; all one really needs to make a beginning is a group of willing students, a teacher who has a sincere desire to involve students in meaningful learning experiences, space enough for children to move freely, and an idea from which to create. A common experience in schools which foster creative expression is that creative activities such as drama, far from consuming energy and leaving students drained, seem actually to release energy so that the child who does the most is often the one who can do more.[42]

And so it seems that we should explore the ideas behind children's drama more carefully. The recommendation of the Social Environment Forum on Leisure in the Arts at the 1960 White House Conference on Children and Youth was "that public and voluntary agencies, schools, colleges and communities provide all children and youth with opportunities to participate in creative dramatics. . . ."[43] In 1966 the participants in the Anglo-American Seminar on the Teaching of English held at Dartmouth College for American and British educators offered the following guidelines for the use of drama and oral communication in the classroom:

1. Drama and oral communication should become the centrality of pupil's exploring, extending, and shaping of experience in the classroom.
2. There is a definite urgency for developing classroom approaches stressing the vital, creative, dramatic involvement of young people in language experiences.
3. The importance of directing more attention to speaking and listening for pupils at all levels, particularly in those experi-

ences which involve vigorous interaction among children, should be apparent.

4. The wisdom of providing young people at all levels with significant opportunities for the creative use of language—creative dramatics, imaginative writing, improvisation, role playing, and similar activities—has become increasingly evident.[44]

It appears, then, that some progress is being made as people become more aware of what Hughes Mearns in *The Creative Adult* called "contagion of the mind, spirit acting upon spirit; it is an important instrument of education; perhaps it is the only important one."[45] Children's drama by its very nature fosters such a "contagion of the mind"; a better reason for including both creative dramatics and children's theater in the curriculum would be hard to find.

Notes

1. Sheridan, "Creative Language Experiences in High School," p. 564.
2. Boyd, "Role Playing," p. 269.
3. As cited in Dearborn, *The Oswego Movement in American Education,* p. 52.
4. Cited in ibid., p. 69. These aspects of Pestalozzi's theory were found in E. A. Sheldon's notebooks.
5. Sheldon, *A Manual of Elementary Instruction,* p. 395.
6. Popovich, *A Study of Significant Contributions to the Development of Creative Dramatics in American Education,* p. 47.
7. Parker, *Talks on Pedagogics,* p. 119.
8. Ibid., p. 7.
9. Putnam, "Faculty Discussions of School Plays," p. 75. The journal *Francis W. Parker Studies in Education* appeared from 1912 to 1934 and carried numerous articles about drama in the schools.
10. DeNeler, "The Central Point of the Platoon School," p. 154.
11. Northwestern University, *Annual Announcement: School of Speech, 1938-39,* p. 41.
12. A normal school was established in 1867 at Oswego, New York, by Sheldon for the purpose of training teachers in the Pestalozzian methods.
13. Popovich, *A Study of Significant Contributions,* p. 136.
14. Originally the book was titled *Creative Drama,* but this was changed to avoid confusion with another book published at the same time: Corinne Brown, *Creative Drama in the Lower School* (1929).
15. Popovich, *A Study of Significant Contributions,* p. 142.
16. Ward, *Playmaking with Children,* pp. 17-22.
17. Merrill was a faculty member of the Francis W. Parker School in Chicago.
18. Heathcote, "Drama," p. 140.
19. Siks, *Creative Dramatics: An Art for Children,* p. 90.
20. McCaslin, *Creative Dramatics in the Classroom,* p. 6.
21. Coggin, *Uses of Drama,* p. 260.
22. Eek, "Theatre, Children's," p. 228.
23. Ibid., p. 229.
24. Ibid., p. 228.
25. Dorothy T. Schwartz, "Development of the Children's Theatre Conference," p. 13.

26. Eek, "Theatre, Children's," p. 230.
27. See Hoetker, *Students as Audiences: An Experimental Study of the Relationships between Classroom Study of Drama and Attendance at the Theatre.* This report presents interesting details about theater going and drama appreciation.
28. Henry, "The Need for Creative Experiences in Oral Language," p. 9.
29. Ward, *Creative Dramatics for the Upper Grades,* p. 3.
30. Siks, *Creative Dramatics,* p. 19.
31. Coggin, *Uses of Drama,* p. 239.
32. Moreno, *The Theatre of Spontaneity,* p. 31.
33. Side, "Creative Drama," p. 431.
34. Corinne Brown, *Creative Drama in the Lower School,* p. 211.
35. Ward, "Creative versus Formal Dramatics," p. 4.
36. Bertram, "Creative Dramatics in the School," p. 517.
37. Ward, *Theatre for Children,* p. 170.
38. Northwestern University, *Annual Announcement: School of Speech, 1926,* p. 23.
39. Siks, *Creative Dramatics,* p. 109.
40. Eek, "Theatre, Children's," p. 228. See also *Directory of American Colleges and Universities Offering Training in Children's Theatre and Creative Dramatics,* rev. ed.
41. See Peluso, *A Survey of the Status of Theatre in United States High Schools.* See also Squire and Applebee, *High School English Instruction Today,* pp. 44-52, and Squire and Applebee, *Teaching English in the United Kingdom,* chapter 4, for contrast in attitudes toward the use of dramatic activity in the schools.
42. Coggin, *Uses of Drama,* p. 229.
43. Siks, "An Appraisal of Creative Dramatics," p. 329.
44. Christensen, "School Drama," p. 33
45. Mearns, *The Creative Adult,* p. 208.

3 Creative Dramatics and the Development of the Child

Jean Piaget has indicated that each of us has a need to forge out of direct experience a mental scheme of the world that has a definite hierarchy of meanings. In a sense this is what the learner proceeds to do as he organizes material and his own behavior, adapting and being adapted as he develops.[1] The individual learns through his activity and through it shapes his own miniature universe which he must somehow place in a much larger framework. This gradual development is marked by a great deal of joy and excitement as well as frustration and disappointment, particularly in a young child.

The joy of discovery in a small child often becomes linked with dramatic play because play is a means of exploration and development as well as being a creation of the moment. Sometimes the energy of the play and the particular moment is interrupted and lost, but the child quickly finds a new experience with which to continue his learning. The essential fragility of discovery through dramatic play offers a good reason for placing emphasis in education on child-centered activities rather than on spectator or audience roles. Only through secure yet active participation will the child be encouraged to discover on his own. This is one of the principal reasons for involving the child in creative dramatics, since here he becomes the center of the action, drawing upon and using his accumulated experiences while exploring primarily for himself and according to his own standards.

As has been previously suggested, creative dramatics offers a way by which children can discover the real world in which they live; they can discover the friendliness of others as well as the sense of magic and love that resides within the souls of all of us. Yet the dramatic event is not meant to be a substitute for an actual experience; instead, drama offers

33

a means by which an experience can be augmented and clarified, focusing the child's attention on the essence of the experience while stripping away the myriad circumstances which normally accompany similar experiences in life.

Participation in creative dramatic activity has many values for the child. We know that it is a part of human nature for a child to desire to be active. He delights in testing new found physical abilities against challenges from the environment. In creative dramatics a child's body becomes a medium through which he creates; he becomes aware of the need for disciplined control as he attempts to coordinate body, mind, and emotions in the expression of ideas, actions, and characters.

Curiosity is another basic characteristic of the child; he revels in his new world, full of mysterious and yet tantalizing events. He learns to look, listen, see, hear, and feel. Active participation in experiences such as are found in most creative dramatic activities calls upon these abilities and helps him to become more responsive to the world around him. As he confronts each new experience he learns the necessity of evaluating and thinking through his reactions. Ultimately through such experiences his social attitudes and appreciations begin to form.

But the child does not remain alone; interaction with others presents new challenges and experiences, and group effort becomes an important factor in his life. Creative dramatic activity provides a multitude of opportunities for interaction and cooperation. Discussions of actions, characterizations, and responses help to develop social awareness and responsibility. The child comes to know what is good and what is bad in portrayal, but he also learns through interaction how to present his responses to others.[2]

The child's development of confidence in himself and in his relationships with others is an important aspect of creative drama, for the student gradually learns to enjoy rather than fear the opportunities to stand up and share his ideas, opinions, and views. A child expresses himself, after all, for the same reasons that men and women of all ages have expressed themselves: he has something to communicate. Consequently, each child is encouraged to reach within himself to express, either through words or actions or both, what he feels and believes. Individuality is constantly encouraged, recognized, and developed, but students enacting a story or a poem have also to deal specifically with problems of egocentricity because differences in understanding arise and have to be resolved.

Identity is important to the young person because he needs to feel important to himself as well as to others. Frequently the release and recognition of identity are important to continuous development, particularly if such recognition does not exist elsewhere in the child's life. Participation in creative drama activities offers at least one source for such recognition.

Creative drama addresses itself to other needs of the child as well. Although learning to distinguish the real from the unreal is a major developmental task of childhood, the individual student is faced with many other equally important tasks. George and Fannie Shaftel have identified a number of these important adjustments which face students of different age levels.

Primary Grades: 5—8 years

1. Learning to adjust to the larger play group of the school
2. Understanding the role of the teacher; sharing an adult with many other children
3. Learning to share toys and other materials
4. Learning to take one's turn and to wait
5. Learning that other people can do things differently and still be all right
6. Learning to relate emotionally to others outside the family group.

Middle Grades: 9—11 years

1. Exploring a wider world
2. Acquiring a basic sense of what is right and what is wrong
3. Learning how to approach strangers and new social situations
4. Seeing family and social groups in relation to others in the community
5. Exploring new emotions: friendship, affection for others, leaving home, death, separation.

Early Adolescence: 12—14 years

1. Adjusting to changes in the body
2. Recognizing the new definitions of boy-girl relationships
3. Learning about one's growth pattern and accepting any personal deviation from the ideal type
4. Moving from neighborhood gang to friendship group based on mutual interests
5. Learning the social definitions of who may or may not be potential friends
6. Being able to handle adequately the demands of parents and the pressures of the peer group.

Later Adolescence: 15—18 years

1. Learning skills in boy-girl relationships in social situations
2. Learning which group values to accept and which to reject
3. Learning the social hierarchy of the community: who "rates" and who does not
4. Developing a social conscience, an awareness of needs and problems of others

5. Finding ways of being successful that are personally satisfying and socially acceptable

6. Acquiring a clear concept of social role and social status of own family and group

7. Learning what rules of social conduct and personal behavior apply in what situation.[3]

From such a list as this we can catch a glimpse of the cumulative effect these tasks may have on students. We can begin to recognize students' needs for secure experiences in which such relationships can be explored and tested and in which appropriate individual roles can be developed. The entire school program should offer experiences which help students come to understand these tasks; creative dramatics provides at least one way of meeting such a challenge, no matter what the subject area.

We can see without too much difficulty that many of the overall objectives of modern education are similar to those of creative dramatics. Geraldine Brain Siks suggests four fundamental educational objectives that creative dramatics constantly emphasizes. They are (1) providing for self-realization in unified learning experiences; (2) offering first-hand experiences in democratic behavior; (3) providing for functional learning which is related to life; and (4) contributing to learning which is comprehensive in scope.[4]

With these objectives common to creative drama and the whole of education, it may be tempting to assume that creative drama should become the cart horse for every subject in the curriculum. Such a view would be naive and could cause irreparable harm to students. If the educative process ceases to relate existence to life and becomes merely a game with no meaning, then the creation and manipulation of an illusion of reality pervert a teacher's power and a student's learning. Too often educational methods and processes are adopted without full knowledge of their uses or limitations, and creative dramatics can be misued as easily as any other approach to learning. Manipulating or influencing others so they will behave in ways primarily satisfying the ego needs of the initiator must be rejected. However, if viable alternatives and a supportive atmosphere for exploration are present, then intentionally simulating reality for a recognized educative purpose can increase learning options for both students and teacher. Acceptable and beneficial approaches to creative drama must emphasize those "strategies, structures or acts which are directed primarily toward the growth of others."[5]

Dangerous, too, is the assumption that creative dramatics is a cure for all disciplinary and emotional problems which occur in the classroom. Forcing children to practice under guidance and pressure the worst sort of personality traits in the guise that "it's only play" can cause continuing personality and behavior problems. Emotional therapy based on an inadequate knowledge of the motives underlying conduct may have far-reaching negative effects on the individual. In working with such areas as drama we must be alert to the idea that nonverbal educational techniques are based on the fact that a child learns most of his emotional response patterns at a very early age—even before he can talk. Hence his knowledge of emotions such as fear, hate, and love comes from the actual feeling and not the verbal symbol. The confusion which can occur as a result of not separating symbol from reality is not desirable educationally.

In light of these dangers, one should remember that creative dramatics is essentially an art form and as such should remain an esthetic experience for children.[6] This esthetic experience, however, can help children develop confidence and a sense of responsibility to others at a time when growing independence could mean insecurity and selfishness toward peers. Significantly, other subjects which attempt to foster this responsibility rely almost exclusively on class discussions, meaning that only one person at a time is recognized. This practice gives ample opportunity for students to hide their feelings and their questions. But drama is action, and it is easy to observe who is not participating; attempts then can be made to encourage but never force the individual to join in group activities and become in this way an integral part of the group's dynamics.

Educators have come to realize that dramatics provides a "preverbal way of understanding, expressing, and representing that underpins not only literacy but oral speech as well."[7] Improvised situations encourage the development of fluency in language, a tolerance for varying points of view, and the beginning of discrimination in the uses of all forms of media.[8]

The provision, too, for controlled emotional release is always present. We have often concerned ourselves in the schools with physical release via elaborate physical education programs and organized sports. The emphasis, however, upon strength and other kinds of physical efficiency seems to have limited relevance to daily living and has small impact upon personality development.[9] In most schools, physical education programs do not provide daily programs of physical exercise. Students find it exceedingly difficult to remain stationary for five to seven hours a day. Activity is a natural desire of the human body, and classroom disciplinary problems often arise from a lack of attention to this function. Creative drama offers one healthy and constructive way to cope with this problem.

All these values inherent in creative drama are summarized by James Moffett when he indicates the purposes of what he calls "acting out":

1. To promote expression of all kinds, movement and speech harmonizing and reinforcing each other
2. To limber body, mind, and tongue

3. To begin to single out the verbal mode from the others and thus to activate speech in particular
4. To forge drama into a learning instrument for continued use throughout the grades
5. To make school experiences with language fun and meaningful in children's terms
6. To habituate pupils to work autonomously in small groups
7. To further peer socialization of a learning sort not possible outside of school
8. To gain intuitive understanding of style as voice, role, and stance and of rhetoric as achieving effect on others
9. To develop in the more familiar mode of dramatic play those characteristics necessary for the less familiar process of discussing, such as attending, responding, interacting, and turn-taking
10. To exercise and channel emotions.[10]

Understandably, Moffett does not visualize that all of these purposes will be achieved at once. Instead he envisions their being introduced and carried on from the moment the child enters school right through his last days in formal education. Actually such a program of development is not so unusual nor difficult as it might seem at first glance if one remembers that most children come to school with the dramatic impulse already. What we attempt to do is to develop this dramatic impulse and thereby foster the growth of creative individuals.

Therapeutic Values of Creative Dramatics

Most of our focus up to this point has been upon the social or academic values of creative drama. Not to be overlooked, however, are the therapeutic values of participating in dramatic activities. Leaders in the field cautiously suggest that creative drama can have some therapeutic value, but they are most reluctant to see the artistic aspects of drama turned into simply another diagnostic or evaluative tool. Yet all authorities in creative dramatics recognize that participation, just as in any other art, can have a beneficial effect upon a person. Most people working with students in creative drama have at one time or another seen individuals and even groups move toward more stability and better emotional health as a result of taking part in such activities.[11]

Psychologists have used dramatic play for some time as a means for observing children's behavior because dramatic play can provide a nonthreatening outlet for emotional disorders which may be causing personality problems.[12] In dramatizations of any type, characters are called upon to show feelings. The child who wants friends but does not know how to win them, for example, often lacks the necessary sensitivity to know what others are thinking by the way they look or act. The child attempting to project himself into another personality has to think about how the other person feels and about how that person shows those feelings. Experiences with this type of projection often help students make better personal adjustments.[13]

Creative drama can have a positive influence on the student who ordinarily fails to receive the recognition he needs so badly. This student will frequently resort to any means he can think of to attract attention. Playmaking serves as a legitimate means for getting attention, but it also demands that one learn to take his turn, to select small parts as well as large ones, and to work within a group. The show-off usually finds that working within the group garners him more attention with positive effect than trying to stay on the outside.

The timid child is another who benefits from exposure to creative dramatics. Usually such a child has an inhibiting image of himself. Obviously he needs encouragement; if the teacher can so stir this child's imagination about a character in a story or a situation that the child feels the urge to play the part, a mild degree of success will often induce him to volunteer for other roles. Playing a number of parts may improve his self-image and lead him to recognize new potentials in himself.[14]

Drama is often recommended for slow learners because these children are not necessarily backward in esthetic appreciation and are therefore highly susceptible to music and drama, especially if they can actively participate. Responses to both rhythm and movement may help to strengthen and coordinate mind and character as well as the body.[15]

Although creative dramatics has been introduced to programs for the speech handicapped (see chapter 4), research suggests that little is being done to provide experiences in creative dramatic activity for other handicapped students. Programs for the visually handicapped and physically handicapped appear only infrequently. The visually handicapped are usually integrated within the regular creative dramatics program. Some adjustments are made but the regular principles and procedures are normally followed without apparent adverse effect upon the children. In at least one instance a "buddy" system was developed that fostered an even closer feeling within the participating group.[16]

For the physically handicapped, adaptations are made according to the type and degree of the handicap. Puppets and shadow plays are often used with these children, but activities also range from simple pantomimes to full creative group action. Volunteers in hospitals have found that children respond quite eagerly to creative drama experiences in which they discover opportunities to project beyond themselves and to forget some of the pain and uncertainty which often accompany a handicap. Again, such work as has been done with the physically handicapped seems to be on a limited scale, and adequate research is lacking in the field.[17]

The education of the gifted child is an area that seems to be overlooked when dealing with creative drama. Great potential exists here because the intellectually gifted child, particularly the ten to twelve year old, needs creative dramatics even more than the child of average intelligence. The gifted child frequently strives for some high degree of perfection, and this can create considerable tension in the individual. Creative dramatics often helps to free and ease the tension in a child who is anxious about doing well. When he becomes physically relaxed, when there is no mark to strive for, no external challenge to better, he can become free to express what he sees and feels. Once the barriers of competition have been erased, there is little stopping the wealth of creativity that flows from such children.[18]

Finally, the application of creative dramatics to the treatment of juvenile delinquency seems possible. Joseph Lee in *Play in Education* stresses that "there is a theatrical element—a half real, half symbolic quality—in a great part of gang activity which makes acting an instinctive method of expression."[19] Peter Slade, an Englishman who has spent considerable time observing children's growth through dramatic play, suggests that possibly "one of the most important reasons for developing child drama in schools generally is not actually a therapeutic one but the even more constructive one of prevention."[20]

It is obvious that these suggestions about the possible applications and benefits of creative drama have definite implications for the community as well as the school, for what is not taken care of in the schools undoubtedly will spill over into the streets. Just that point was made in the report of the First International Conference on Theatre and Youth sponsored by the United States Commission for UNESCO in 1952. The Conference's report claimed the following:

> . . . juvenile delinquency and vandalism can be lessened in communities everywhere if leisure-time youth programs are challenging enough to bring children from the streets. Creative dramatics offers an active program whereby children are given a chance to "blow off steam," where feelings are expressed rather than suppressed, and where boys and girls find pleasure working together. . . .[21]

But such pronouncements have made little evident impression. The lack of widespread research in the areas previously mentioned shows this; because of the lack of interest, little concrete evidence has been accumulated to support requests for appropriate programs. Some scattered programs exist, particularly with disadvantaged youth, and in most instances the results have been promising but not highly publicized.[22] We must consider, however, that the necessary ingredients are present for work with creative drama in all of these areas. When the dynamic powers of childhood imagination and creativity are channeled into strong and constructive activities, the results can only be of great benefit to the children immediately and to the community at large in the future.

Creative drama offers strong contributions in promoting social adjustment, stimulating creative expression, and fostering a greater awareness of and sensitivity to environment and human interaction. That creative drama is not a panacea for all personality and disciplinary problems, slow learning, or lack of creativity should be evident. Creative drama does, nevertheless, offer the individual teacher a number of flexible approaches from which to work as he strives to meet the various needs of his individual students.

Notes

1. Featherstone, "How Children Learn," p. 18.
2. Slade, *Child Drama,* p. 58.
3. Shaftel and Shaftel, *Role Playing the Problem Story,* pp. 40-41. Reprinted by permission of the National Conference of Christians and Jews.
4. Siks, *Creative Dramatics,* p. 41.
5. George I. Brown, *Human Teaching for Human Learning,* p. 240.
6. Bertram, "Creative Dramatics in the School," pp. 517-18.
7. Moffett, *A Student-Centered Language Arts Curriculum,* p. 33.
8. "Drama Is the Key," p. 1937.
9. Creber, *Sense and Sensitivity,* p. 97.
10. Moffett, *A Student-Centered Language Arts Curriculum,* pp. 35-36. Reprinted by permission of Houghton Mifflin Company.
11. York, "Values to Children from Creative Dramatics," pp. 128-29.
12. Ward, *Playmaking with Children,* p. 213. For short, interesting accounts of the use of drama in psychology, see Barbato, "Drama Therapy," and Slade, *Child Drama,* pp. 116-22.
13. Ward, *Playmaking with Children,* pp. 214-15.
14. Ibid., pp. 210-11.
15. Coggin, *Uses of Drama,* p. 235. See also Ebbitt, "Drama for Slow Learners," Hawkes, "Dramatic Work for Backward Children," and Keyes, "Creative Dramatics and the Slow Learner."
16. McIntyre, "Creative Dramatics Programs for Exceptional Children," p. 156.
17. Ibid. For fuller discussion and case studies see Schattner, *Creative Dramatics for Handicapped Children,* and Robert Chambers, *Creative Dramatics, Learning or Play?*
18. Senderowitz, "How One Community Uses Creative Dramatics," p. 27.
19. Joseph Lee, *Play in Education,* p. 363. See also Downs and Pitkanen, "Therapeutics Dramatics for Delinquent Boys."
20. Slade, *Child Drama,* p. 119.
21. Cited in Siks, *Creative Dramatics,* p. 43.
22. Gray, "The Pennsylvania Advancement School," pp. 306-21.

4 Special Areas and Applications of Drama in Education

Twentieth century society has long sought to provide for each individual an education which will harmonize with his native capacities. Unfortunately, many thousands of youngsters, because of their inheritances or the influence of their environments, can profit very little from what the average school has to offer. Periodically extra amounts of money and attention are given these children, but the lack of consistent programs for them as well as the absence of sufficient numbers of trained personnel means that in most instances these children receive an inferior education.

Creative Dramatics and Mental Disabilities

All people desire to create. Although retarded children are not creative in the general sense of the word, they have definite aptitudes for certain types of creative expression. As a rule they will not originate ideas and execute them, but they enjoy "doing" something themselves. Most state education codes define educable mentally retarded children as those individuals who are incapable of coping with normal class programs. Yet these people can still profit from special education programs designed to make them economically useful and socially adjusted individuals.[1]

The retarded tend to learn more slowly and retain less factual information than regular students, but the retarded still use the processes of imitation, reasoning, and generalization.[2] Teachers working with such students find that dramatic play can be a useful approach to learning; it is a natural and flexible approach which stimulates language and fosters the formation and growth of personality patterns. But play becomes a source of information as well as a part of personality development. Hence the basic principles and practices of creative dramatics which pertain to the average child appear to be similarly effective with retarded children.

Some discrimination must be made, however, as to the needs of each child. To expect verbal communication, insights, and all the other aspects of play activity to occur with the retarded child at equal levels is naive. The mentally retarded frequently need more sense of structure than regular students. They need certain kinds of stimulation and motivation in order to understand abstractions. The use of small informal groups helps such pupils begin to verbalize. For example, students may be given different objects to examine, then asked to mime as many uses of the objects as they can while other students react. This type of activity leads to discussion of qualities as well as uses and eventually helps the individuals work together as a group.

Because of his limitations, though, a retarded child seldom joins a group spontaneously. He is similar to a very young child who plays alone and has to learn to enjoy the people who are around him. A retarded child must work into a group situation gradually. The first step in this direction usually occurs within the family; this is followed by a play group and then perhaps the school and society at large. It is recommended that eight children be the maximum number in any group. Often the teacher will need to act with the children in order to stimulate their activity and to let them feel that everyone is working together. The retarded child enjoys repetition and needs it to gain confidence in himself, so many experiences will be repeated until the child shows a satisfactory degree of confidence in his behavior.[3]

A great amount of understanding and patience is called for when working with these children. Adults find it difficult to believe that a boy with a chronological age of twelve but a mental age of three will respond to the same activities that a normal three year old enjoys.[4] Creative dramatic activities help to simplify life and character while coordinating many items into one focus. For the very slow, inhibited child, action-pictures in the form of dramatic playlets seem to brighten the mental images and make them more lasting.[5] Usually there are signs of enlarged vocabulary and an increased social and emotional poise as well as expressions of happiness in being allowed to participate in such stimulating fun.[6]

The application and use of creative drama with mentally retarded students, then, should follow the general principles indicated below:

1. Each child should be offered opportunities for participation in group activity.
2. Creative drama with retarded children should be a guided activity, not a directed one.

3. Participation in creative dramatics should help such children learn the positive advantages of social cooperation.
4. Participation in creative dramatics provides the retarded child with opportunities for emotional release.
5. Dramatic activity frees the retarded child from emphasis upon spectator situations.[7]

Creative Dramatics and Speech Disabilities

Most children with retarded mental development also have speech difficulties, many of which center on articulatory defects. The desire to take part in dramatic activity makes these children more conscious of their speech problems and provides a certain motivation to improve. "The use of creative dramatics for speech correction is based on the assumption that it is a variable and pleasurable technique which offers a strong incentive for the cultivation of good speech, because the children themselves realize that they must be heard and understood just as they demand that others make themselves heard and understood."[8] Hence two basic advantages are present with the use of creative drama in the speech program: (1) it is an activity with speech as a core—planning, discussing, playmaking, and evaluating; (2) spontaneous and free speech is encouraged.

Otto Jespersen reminds us that without speech we would find daily life almost impossible; we take the act of speech so much for granted that we tend to forget the struggle and fear that children with speech handicaps must undergo. As Jespersen says:

> In our so-called civilized life print plays such an important part that educated people are apt to forget that language is primarily speech, that is, chiefly conversation (dialogue), while the written (and printed) word is only a kind of substitute—in many ways a most valuable one, but in other respects a poor one—for the spoken and heard word. Many things that have vital importance in speech—stress, pitch, colour of the voice, thus especially those elements which give expression to emotions rather than to logical thinking—disappear in the comparatively rigid medium of writing, or are imperfectly rendered by such means as underlining (italicizing) and punctuation. What is called the life of language consists in oral intercourse with its continual give-and-take between speaker and hearer.[9]

The importance of speech in the everyday functioning of the individual may move the speech clinic to suggest that a child be involved in creative dramatics. Normally, creative drama in the speech clinic is used as an adjunct to therapy in order to provide successful speaking experiences or as a technique to stimulate auditory training. However, research suggests that the articulation skills of some children can be improved by their participation in dramatic activity in the regular classroom. The trained speech therapist does not expect the regular classroom teacher to be a clinician. He does, however, expect that the regular teacher will be a competent facilitator of dramatic activity which will provide experiences and an atmosphere conducive to creative expression. Emphasis usually is placed on rhythms of speech, speech sounds, and word attack skills. Students are encouraged to supply sounds to match narratives and to help each other with the recognition of new sounds as they are encountered. More needs to be done in this area before specific claims can be made regarding the lasting effects of such training, but preliminary experiments have been quite promising.[10]

Barbara McIntyre in her study of a group of children between the ages of ten and fourteen found, during a six-week creative activities program where no unusual emphasis was placed upon developing articulatory skills, that the number of articulation errors in children's speech was significantly reduced.[11] In another study, Charlotte Ludwig showed that a group of kindergarten pupils who were exposed to the medium of creative dramatics for a period of three months made significantly greater improvements in articulation than did the control group.[12]

Such research suggests that programs which use creative drama as a focal point can be developed to foster improved speech performance. Such programs would include ear training, reinforcement of sound through many sensory and motor approaches, the use of sound in carefully prepared and controlled speaking situations, and finally a carry-over of sounds into every life situation.[13]

To begin with, ear training focuses on four areas: (1) hearing a sound in isolation; (2) hearing the sound frequently; (3) identifying characteristics of the correct sound; and (4) discriminating one sound from another sound. In achieving these various aspects of ear training, the teacher will find that some of the approaches used on television programs such as *Sesame Street* and *The Electric Company* provide excellent materials; also riddles, jingles, stories, and poems which stress particular sounds in isolation will be helpful. By telling stories and then having the children enact them—supplying the proper sounds as they perform—the teacher will be engaging students in activities which begin to help students focus on the articulation of particular sounds. If mirrors are used, students can see how a sound is shaped and can then help each other make the proper movements for the sound in question. Selecting and naming objects which begin with a certain sound, such as "b" for "bell," give children additional practice. The teacher may read a story, and each time the children hear the sound they raise their hands; this provides a good evaluation check on students' progress.[14]

A critical step in developing speech skills is the reinforcement of sound training. Certain sound sequences can be worked into playmaking situations, such as a scene where animals are talking to each other in their own language. Another approach is found in the game "King Knowledge" developed by Rita Criste of the Evanston schools in Illinois. She worked with sixth grade students in developing the following story: a group of children wishing to eliminate some vowel sounds petitioned King Knowledge to remove a few. After the children had an audience with the king to present the petition, he called in each of the vowels separately to let everyone justify his existence. At this point each child made up words incorporating the sounds which were being examined. Depending upon the cleverness of the words, verdicts were rendered as to which sounds would remain and which would go.[15]

Eventually, if ear training has been successful, students will begin to learn sounds merely by listening to them. Discussion initiated to bring about the usage of specific words or sounds is also helpful. Students can enact stories which have several different kinds of characters calling for a wide range of tone among the various parts. The most natural way to introduce characterization and dialogue is through rhythm. Using rhymes, the teacher encourages the students to chant sounds together and to begin to listen for changes in tone and pace. This activity can lead into a type of improvisation with dialogue, sparked by questions such as "What kind of voice does Mrs. Spider have?" or "Where has Miss Muffet been?" Many children who have trouble during regular conversation speak fluently when they are playing a character. Moving back and forth between real-life roles and fictive ones helps to develop continuity in speech patterns and gives the child more security as he tests his abilities.

Students definitely profit from the combination of speech training and creative drama. Pierini found that in fifteen meetings with students in which she emphasized speech skills within a creative dramatic framework, the following results were achieved:

1. Students exhibited more care in speaking clearly.
2. Greater poise and control appeared in speaking.
3. Words followed more freely in conversation.
4. Students exhibited more readiness and willingness to contribute to the subject under discussion.
5. Observable increases appeared in terms of a more acute listening sense.
6. Increases in vocabulary occurred.
7. Correction of certain sounds and strengthening of others were apparent.[16]

Creative dramatics and speech therapy complement each other. Creative drama provides a framework within which students with defective speech can actively engage in enjoyable speaking situations which offer opportunities for correction and drill on specific defects.

Dramatic activity also capitalizes on the relationship between interest and learning. "Language gains reality and impact which ordinary classroom interchange simply does not effect. Improvised drama permits a free exploration of the potentialities of the intonations, sounds, and rhythms of language."[17]

Psychodrama and Emotional Problems

Many children have a very limited ability to communicate in words their feelings about problems with social relationships. Consequently, Jacob L. Moreno, a well-known psychotherapist, has suggested that every public school, elementary and secondary, as well as every college should provide for the use of psychodrama as a guidance laboratory for students' everyday problems. The term "psychodrama" as coined by Dr. Moreno is derived from the Greek word *psyche* meaning "mind" or "soul" and *dramein* meaning "to do" or "to act." In combination, the term refers to an individual's expression of his intellectual and emotional processes, not only through speech but also through movement and gesture.[18]

Basically three main types of psychodrama are available. Diagnostic psychodrama is a research tool; it provides a method for analyzing groups and individuals regarding their potential for various types of future action. An example of this would be the analysis of a mental patient's behavior in certain situations for the purpose of determining whether he is ready for release from an institution. Therapeutic psychodrama, on the other hand, emphasizes the correction of functional disorders of a non-somatic origin. Focus is placed on various types of blocks, frustrations, or inhibitions with the intent that dramatic catharsis will help to clear such blocks away and healthy, integrated actions will take their place. Educational psychodrama concerns itself with the control and direction of normal behavior toward desired goals; hence the particular contribution of educational psychodrama is the improvement of present behavior patterns.[19]

The use of psychodrama, therefore, is not restricted to those individuals whose problems are pathological. Instead, psychodrama offers a type of training in acting out past and present problems, both realistically and symbolically, both alone and with others. The spontaneity and awareness which spring from such activity benefit perfectly normal people as well as those with more deep-seated difficulties. According to Samuel Kahn, in psychodrama,

> the actual drama lies in the confrontation of the unconscious attitudes and wishes by the objective reality of the situation. The drama becomes a concrete form of reality-testing. The protagonist literally sees that there may be other ways than his own of reacting to a given situation, and as he tries them out on the

stage, he begins to understand his effect on people around him and to integrate his new knowledge into behavior that is based on a clearer perception of the realities of any situation.[20]

The applications of educational psychodrama are numerous. It can be helpful in meeting situations such as overcoming a deep-set fear, improving social behavior techniques, understanding and accepting physical and mental abnormalities in other children, and meeting daily frustrations in the home, school, and neighborhood. Those children who benefit most from psychodrama seem to have certain general characteristics in common. They tend to be unable to engage in anticipatory thinking; they are overwhelmed by new or recurring situations where demands are felt to be too complex to handle; and they are often incapable of achieving success because of their fear of separation from or the antagonism of certain key figures in their lives, such as parents, teachers, or friends.[21] For instance, children with emotional difficulties may create characters which will enable them to vent feelings. One girl of ten always wished to play mean parts. She would play witches, goblins, the mean sister, or the wicked stepmother with great vigor. One day a teacher asked her if she would like to play the part of Cinderella. The girl smiled and said, "No, that's what I have to be at home." She lived with her parents, grandparents, and two aunts, and was the pride of the family. Creative drama functioned as a release for her and helped her to meet other pressures placed upon her.[22]

The person using psychodramatic techniques usually finds himself with children who are ready to act out various themes but who have no conception of how to find help on a certain problem. It is very rare that one goes into an episode from a diagnostic discussion of the problem; this approach should be discouraged, especially with young children. Much more frequently a teacher will find that the problem theme emerges from a child's choice of activities. For instance, a child may be terribly afraid of fire; dramatizing situations with him which involve fires of various types and in which he may play different roles such as the fire chief, big brother protecting baby sister, or father taking care of the family will help the student to gradually overcome his fear.[23]

Psychodrama is generally applied in situations which include admitted personal-problem situations or which involve unresolved conflicts with adult figures or peers. General social situations involving lack of social skills or problems of conscious or unconscious prejudice are other potential areas.

Psychodramatic episodes with preschool children must include clear demonstrations of cause and effect. This relationship must be communicated in the action rather than by any attempts at verbal interpretation after the fact. For this reason the use of psychodrama in the home, with the parents playing various adult roles, seems to make it possible for the parents to transfer a sense of emotional warmth to other adult-child relationships, such as the teacher-child, policeman-child type of association.[24]

Psychodrama in its broad sense and as it applies to education is a whole family of skills, techniques, and processes involved in the unrehearsed but not unplanned dramatization of human problems for the purpose of dealing with them more effectively. In this sense, then, creative drama and psychodrama are closely related, for many creative dramatic techniques are employed in psychodrama. Caution should be exercised, however, to see that psychodrama, when attempted by parents and educators, is used for educational purposes. The diagnostic and therapeutic types of psychodrama should be reserved for the trained psychiatrist and clinician. Paul Goodman, noted critic of education, has nevertheless recommended that educators pay more attention to psychotherapy and its application to education.

> Teaching small children is a difficult art, but we do not know how to train the improvisational genius it requires . . . since at this age one teaches the child, not the subject. The relevant art is psychotherapy and the most useful course for a normal school is probably group therapy.[25]

Games and Simulations

We have shown several times that conflict is the essence of drama; conflict is also a major part of the life of man. We live on an increasingly crowded planet with widely divergent life styles growing out of an increasingly complex technology. For some people, the conflicts which arise become insurmountable; for others, conflict is not necessarily an inevitable evil. Students who learn to cope with conflicts induced in simulation and who learn to test methods of competition and cooperation under various conditions can develop into citizens more capable of meeting and dealing with the stresses and strains of everyday human life.

Studies indicate that most children in primitive societies learn by mimetic games. The basic distinction between serious games and childlike games is that serious games rely on knowledge more than imagination. Such games may involve principles or theories that provide the players with explanations of the dimensions of human behavior, mathematics, ecology, or other subjects. The reason why we as adults understand written and spoken representations of these complex interaction processes is that we base our understanding on analogies to direct personal experience. In a sense we simulate the process we are studying by referring to past experiences. However, to an elementary or high school student who does not have sufficient experience to form analogies, abstractions presented the first time without any concrete simulation of their interaction merely remain abstractions.[26]

Playing a game is psychologically different in degree but not in kind from dramatic activity. The ability to create a situation imaginatively and to play a role in it is a rewarding experience—a sort of holiday from one's regular self and the routine of everyday living. Psychological freedom becomes a reality and creates conditions in which strain and conflict are dissolved and potentiality is released in spontaneous efforts to meet the demands of the situation. Any good play contains uncertainty about its outcome because the principal characters are in conflict. The basic requirement, however, is that one care about the characters—they cannot be utterly trivial people. Educational games must be similarly constructed so that all the roles have some fantasy interest for the players and so that the outcome of the interaction is uncertain.

Educational games are a combination of systems analysis and dramatics. The systems analysis is in the design of the game and in the analysis and restatement of the problem in a structured, analytical format. The dramatics comes in selecting those aspects of the situation which are full of conflict and uncertainty and whose outcomes are unknown.[27]

Two general types of simulation exist in education. One is found in board games such as *Monopoly;* basically these are quite weak as learning instruments because the outcomes of the moves are relatively independent of the quality of the decisions made by the players. The other type is a role-play game which is like a partially structured drama whose ending is still uncertain. Here the players and their decisions are an integral part of the outcome of the simulation.

Three kinds of learning take place during the simulation. The student learns the facts of a situation; he comes to see cause and effect relationships; and he contends with comparisons of alternate costs and benefits, risks, and opportunities which would follow different courses of action.[28]

The educational games method of learning is a laboratory approach similar to that used in physics and chemistry labs. Its most immediate application lies in the areas of social science and the humanities, where there is little opportunity in the conventional education program for the student to participate actively in decision making concerning the problems under study.[29]

Educational games provide a natural group format calling for involvement and personal freedom—both essentials for experiencing. When actors participate in a simulated social system by making decisions and arranging for their implementation, the result is a mixture of competition and cooperation typical of the event being studied. Actors must learn the rules, comprehend the essential elements of the environment, understand the implications of the available alternatives, and develop increasingly elaborate strategies of action. Students learn to operate the simulated system in order to gain a better understanding of the dynamics which exist in the macrocosm that lies beyond the classroom.[30]

The development of classroom simulation is still in its infancy, and a great many of the simulations on the market reflect the growing pains of unsound attempts to produce a finished product that is useful to the classroom teacher (see the annotated listing of simulations in part three, "Handbook of Resources"). Simulation is not a panacea for bringing the real world into the classroom. Unless one can find a satisfactory answer to the question, Does the game have a sound knowledge base? then relatively little assurance can be given that the game will contribute effectively to student learning.

The learning principles involved in simulation are attractive to educators and are quite closely related to the principles involved in creative dramatic activities. These common principles include the following:

1. Experiencing the consequences of one's actions helps one to learn.
2. Having a grasp of the complexities of the problems before beginning to tackle them is an asset to the learner; games and drama offer an approximation of the outside world and its problems.
3. Learning takes place more effectively if attention is focused.
4. Placing more emphasis on the student and his responsibilities, and on developing the role of the teacher as guide rather than director, makes learning a more individualized process.
5. Offering players the sense that they have some control over outcomes is important to students, expecially to the culturally disadvantaged.

Using drama and simulation in learning experiences with multiple groups at the same time makes it possible to encompass a wide range of skills. But games, like creative drama and other teaching strategies, should not be embraced as the solution for all problems of instruction. Used with discretion and understanding, simulations offer rewards. However, perhaps the greatest benefits derived from either drama or simulation result from what happens after the playing is over; the discussion of what actually happened, of how realistic it was, of what the strategies and problems were will give the experience much of its meaning.

All special applications of drama in the classroom are important because they provide multiple ways for the teacher and the student to become more involved in the learning process. William Iverson, speaking of these benefits, says:

He [the student] can extend his life space in a hundred different roles. He can achieve an emotional release from the experimentation, sensing the power of the spoken word to stir, to calm, to anger, to mollify. He can be swept by the unpredictable dialogue into trying to find language suited to the feeling context which has that very moment arisen. He can lend tonal vestments to word and utterance in a driving desire to get attuned to the nuances of the relationship being projected. He can, in short, rise to a new perspective on the ways language both facilitates and denies human commonality.[31]

Our basic task in education is to discover appropriate strategies that take individual differences into consideration but that do so in such a way as to foster the development of the individual. Creative drama, with its emphasis on personal involvement and attention to the experiential backgrounds of the participants, offers individuals a wide range of opportunities for discovering and achieving their aspirations. The child, whether he is handicapped or normal, profits from confrontations with practical and social problems as well as with personal issues. Creative drama provides the student with opportunities to learn through doing and to enjoy and know what it feels like to use the creative part of himself.

Notes

1. Rothstein, ed., *Mental Retardation: Readings and Resources,* p. 163.
2. McIntyre, *Informal Dramatics: A Language Arts Activity for the Special Pupil,* p. 27.
3. Senderowitz, "How One Community Uses Creative Dramatics," pp. 21-32.
4. Carlson and Ginglend, *Play Activities for the Retarded Child,* p. 13.
5. Moskowitz, "Dramatics as an Educational Approach to the Mentally Handicapped," p. 215.
6. McIntyre, "Creative Dramatics in Programs for Exceptional Children," p. 155. See also McIntyre, *Informal Dramatics.*
7. McIntyre, *Informal Dramatics,* pp. 7-10.
8. Pierini, *Application of Creative Dramatics to Speech Therapy,* p. 25.
9. Jespersen, *Essentials of English Grammar,* p. 17.
10. McIntyre, "Creative Dramatics in Programs for Exceptional Children," p. 155. See the following: McIntyre and McWilliams, "Creative Dramatics in Speech Correction"; Ludwig, *The Effect of Creative Dramatics Activities upon the Articulation Skills of Kindergarten Children;* McIntyre, *The Effects of a Program of Creative Activities upon the Articulation Skills of Adolescent and Pre-Adolescent Children with Speech Disorders;* and Pierini, *Application of Creative Dramatics to Speech Therapy.*
11. McIntyre, "The Effect of Creative Activities on the Articulation Skills of Children," pp. 42-48.
12. See Ludwig, *The Effect of Creative Dramatics Activities upon the Articulation Skills of Kindergarten Children.*
13. Pierini, *Application of Creative Dramatics to Speech Therapy,* p. 18.
14. Ibid.

15. Popovich, *A Study of Significant Contributions to the Development of Creative Dramatics in American Education,* p. 162.
16. Pierini, *Application of Creative Dramatics to Speech Therapy,* p. 46.
17. Iverson, "The Lively Arts of Language in the Elementary School," p. 84.
18. Kahn, *Psychodrama Explained,* p. 1.
19. Levy, "Psychodrama and the Philosophy of Cultural Education," pp. 226-28.
20. Kahn, *Psychodrama Explained,* p. 35.
21. Eliasoph, "Concepts and Techniques of Role Playing and Role Training Utilizing Psychodramatic Methods in Group Therapy with Adolescent Drug Addicts," p. 308.
22. McIntyre and McWilliams, "Creative Dramatics in Speech Correction," p. 277.
23. See Lippitt, "Psychodrama in the Home."
24. Lippitt, "Psychodrama in the Home," p. 167.
25. As cited in Dennison, *The Lives of Children,* p. 266.
26. Abt, "Games and Simulation," p. 7.
27. Ibid., p. 5.
28. Ibid.
29. Ibid., p. 1.
30. Meir, "Simulations for Transmitting Concepts of Social Organization," pp. 156-75.
31. Iverson, "The Lively Arts of Language in the Elementary School," p. 84.

Participation in any of the arts is . . . more needed today than at any other period in our history. Drama, of all the arts, demands of the practitioner a total involvement. By offering an opportunity for participation in drama, we are helping to preserve something of the play impulse in all of its joy, freedom and order.

Nellie McCaslin, *Creative Dramatics in the Classroom*, p. 154.

5 The Future of Creative Dramatics in Education

Aldous Huxley once pointed out that "all our mental processes depend upon perception. Inadequate perceiving results in poor thinking, inappropriate feeling, diminished interest in and enjoyment of life. Systematic training of perception should be an essential element in all education."[1] It does not take long for us to discover that the solutions to many of life's problems are not strictly individual, internal, or abstract; instead they require "communication to and persuasion of others that one's personal solution is desirable or acceptable. Communication and persuasion require skills of perception, self-expression and negotiation in interpersonal relations—skills seldom taught in schools."[2]

As a country we have developed an astounding worship for what we understand to be science. Mainly as a result of this reverence, we value objectivity and analysis more highly than originality and synthesis. The abilities to prove one's position and to deduce conclusions from premises are thought more important than the abilities to impose new types of structure on experience and to generate new and meaningful points of view and hypotheses. Hence every child needs to learn to communicate and to enjoy speaking, listening, writing, and reading with others.

These needs are one of the principal arguments for the continued and expanded use of creative dramatics in the curriculum, both elementary and secondary. Harold Rugg and Ann Shumaker claim that "drama, more than any other single art, represents an integration of all the processes of self-expression. It is at once the most completely personal, individualistic and intimate as well as the most highly socialized art. Rich in content, varied in means, it represents also an effective union of intellect and emotion."[3]

But creative dramatics does not just happen. Only as far as it is approached with the same seriousness and consciousness of ultimate educational goals as are the traditional pursuits of the school may creative dramatics be expected to justify its presence in educational programs. It is an art which requires careful guidance as well as skilled organization. Guiding children in order to set creative expression in motion and guiding students to opportunities for strong participation are goals common to both education and creative drama.

It should be apparent by now that the basic theory of creative dramatics is not new. Its application within the classroom, particularly in the United States, has not yet achieved widespread acceptance, partly because of educators' ignorance concerning the relationship between creative dramatics and the educational process. The question still arises as to what the distinctive contributions are that creative drama offers to children which justify its inclusion in the curriculum. In reply to this, Philip Coggin in *Uses of Drama* says:

> Creative drama is "the doing of life." Real life experiments may be fatal, costly, or beyond our reach. In drama the whole of life can be lived with all its excitement and none of its danger. Whatever the social circumstances there can be total living, and since drama is also unity in variety, it is a great integrating force. It helps the personality to self-realization by educating the emotions, stimulating the intellect, and co-ordinating movement and gesture to the wishes of the mind and spirit. A fully developed human being is, by definition, a full member of society, and the communal character of drama encourages the full development of the social group. A community spirit founded on principles of truth and sincerity could go far beyond parochial interests to embrace eventually the whole community of mankind.[4]

Although Coggin's claims regarding the efficacy of drama may be somewhat exaggerated, he still has seen the essential ingredients which make drama, and creative drama in particular, an integral part of the educative process.

A second consideration in deciding the future status of creative dramatics in the school centers on whether the art should be taught as a separate subject, as are music and the graphic arts, or integrated with other subject matter. The somewhat varied practices and philosophies in the field tend to confuse educators as to the proper position of creative dramatics in the curriculum. At times the subject is used as an educational technique; at other times it is seen solely as a theater art. In some situations it is considered a separate academic subject,[5] and on still other occasions it is viewed as a personality development strategy.

This flexibility makes creative drama ideal for a variety of programs and hence has led to its multiple uses. But to make drama simply another subject in the already overcrowded curriculum is to shift the emphasis away from people to drama itself, and certainly this was not the intention of Ward, Siks, and others who developed creative drama.

The confusion, however, has prompted those concerned with the future of creative dramatics to suggest steps for clarification. The American Educational Theatre Association (now the American Theatre Association) determined in 1957 certain priorities which it felt were essential if children's drama was to develop in the United States.

1. A need to introduce children's drama training programs at college and university levels and to improve those programs already in existence,
2. A need to strengthen the standards of present children's drama programs by examining and improving basic principles and practices,
3. A need to increase opportunities in school and community programs so that drama becomes accessible to every child,
4. A need to educate the public to the philosophy of children's drama to insure school, community, and national support.[6]

These priorities remain; recent conferences and publications, however, suggest that slowly some gains are being made. Still, the individualized nature of creative drama confuses those curriculum makers who tend to see items in a compartmentalized structure; since creative dramatics crosses boundary lines into all disciplines, it frustrates pigeonholing. A more precise philosophy might help bring the subject into greater demand, but the very nature of creative expression—the heart of creative drama—defies that preciseness. As Dorothy Heathcote says, "A good drama experience cannot either be preserved or transferred easily, so that those using drama intuitively in the classroom find it difficult to communicate what they do to achieve their ends, or the means they employ to learn which ends are relevant at that time and in that particular circumstance."[7]

Theater groups and drama departments throughout the country continue to work toward making the public more aware of what creative drama is. Federal funding has made it possible for groups to work in communities and to expose a large number of people to the values of dramatics. Teachers, too, have been offered workshops which will train them in the fundamentals of creative drama. With continued efforts in these areas and with the support of organizations such as the American Theatre Association and the National Council of Teachers of English, more understanding and backing should be forthcoming from the public as well as from education in general.

That creative drama has multiple uses has drawn increasing attention. Participants in the Anglo-American Seminar at Dartmouth College (1966) were convinced that drama, in the sense of creative dramatics, should be made an integral part of at least the English curriculum, from the beginning to the end.[8] James R. Squire and Roger K. Applebee's study of English teaching in the British Isles, completed in 1969, underscored this position. Observers who visited British schools were impressed by the amount of class time—up to 25 percent—that was given to dramatic activities. In spite of the fact that the British include all speech experiences, excluding regular class discussion, within the designation of dramatic activity,[9] this emphasis was amazing, particularly when compared with findings reported in another study by Squire and Applebee, done in 1968, which investigated the quality of high school English programs in American secondary schools. During this study no actual use of dramatics as a teaching method was observed, and teachers themselves did not list creative dramatics as one of the methods they used most frequently.[10]

The British, however, have developed their programs to the point where creative drama is used on all grade levels and is considered a valuable teaching approach. A great deal of emphasis is placed upon drama as literature, of course, but the widespread reliance on improvised drama was what surprised American observers. The British justify their emphasis in this way:

> The educational value of dramatic play does not diminish in the junior schools but its form will change as the children mature. . . . As from the infant to the junior, so from the junior to the secondary. The forms of drama change; its validity remains. The range of material becomes wider, its treatment more thorough.[11]

During the time American observers were in the British schools they saw students recreating for their own enjoyment and education, not that of an audience, such things as the Aberfan coal-mining disaster in Wales, the response of the population after an atomic holocaust, the killing of Claudius (in *Hamlet*), the Prometheus legend, the story of the Prodigal Son, the construction of Noah's ark, selections from the *Canterbury Tales,* and even the trial, crucifixion, and resurrection of Jesus.[12]

The emphasis in the British report fell on dramatic practices at the secondary level, in direct contrast to American school systems where, for the most part, creative drama has been thought of as a subject suitable only for the elementary grades. Few attempts have been made in this country to develop any continuity from the elementary grades into the junior and senior high schools. Yet many of the problems which begin at the junior high age—destructive rebellion, alienation from school, delinquency and dropping out—can be alleviated if adolescents see school as a place "where feelings and energy can be shaped and handled, instead of a place where these forces must be stifled until time to meet with the gang again."[13]

During the junior high and senior high years, several important shifts take place in dramatic work. First, materials become more complex; students begin to explore more personal areas and become involved in trying to define their roles in society. Second, dramatic work becomes a critical process by which other assignments may be introduced and explored. Enactment and improvisation continue, but the emphasis shifts to a more deliberate examination of topical ideas, and improvisation culminates in the freest of minimal situations. This progress toward integration of other subject fields allows for the continued growth of the individual's creative expression while also broadening his area of participation. In this way school becomes a place where students express themselves and learn to adjust to the pressures and problems that face them outside. Teenagers are much in need of this, and the school is about the only place left where such activity can take place effectively. The social needs for higher quality mass education for those of diverse cultural and ability backgrounds suggest that role playing, gaming, modeling, and simulation may be the most cost-effective educational innovations available to us today.[14]

The present lack of continuity from grade to grade constitutes one of the outstanding weaknesses of creative dramatics from the standpoint of the whole educational program. Ideally, education in creative drama should be cumulative. Unless this becomes a reality, it will be quite difficult for creative dramatics activities to contribute permanently to emotional and linguistic development. Programs for the future must focus on ways to make experiences in improvised drama a part of the mainstream of classroom activity.

It will not be easy for creative drama to achieve this position. American society values drama less fully than does the society of Great Britain, partly because of basic differences in educational philosophies. Americans have thought of drama as performance and as an entertainment medium, and to think of it in terms of personality development will take a considerable adjustment. Play is still thought to be frivolous by those who subscribe to the commonly held work ethic which contends that pleasurable activities are not serious and that true seriousness requires sobriety and even pain on occasion.

The British, on the other hand, steeped as they are in a long tradition of drama, have seen the importance of drama and have moved beyond mere performance to total involvement in everyday life. The resultant effects on students are obvious. Observers during the Squire-Applebee study continually remarked about the confidence and happiness which they saw in the classroom, an air of vitality and interest frequently missing from the American classroom. The British attribute much of this atmosphere to the experiences in drama. It is probably true that an individual develops a feeling for literature as much through kinesthetic activity and association as through more intellectualized approaches; and drama seems to be the most promising vehicle at hand to allow such direct engagement. [15] The implications here suggest that Americans, who have begun to complain about lifelessness and apathy in the classroom, might do well to consider at least more experiments in the uses of drama to see for themselves what the results might be.

Still, we will proceed cautiously if at all. Too often American education has charged ahead only to find that it is going nowhere. Such experiences tend to make us conservative at times and reluctant to change. Change, if it is to come, should be brought about through commitment and involvement, not by edict or revolution. Past history shows that the road to "Hell is paved with good intentions, and whole periods of history have been made hideous or grotesque by enthusiastic idealists who failed to elaborate the means whereby their lofty aspirations might be effectively, and above all, harmlessly implemented."[16]

Educators committed to a more humanistic approach in our schools are realizing that they must show results with sensible programs that illustrate how such things as creative dramatics will help the cause of education. Recent works such as George I. Brown's *Human Teaching for Human Learning: An Introduction to Confluent Education* (1971) show this concern. People are beginning to realize that to engage in change, "there is no magic wand, including the cudgel of violent revolution, that will make the person or institution committed to standing dead still suddenly convert to a passionate course of living, learning and growth."[17] But if the new philosophy, the new approach, will fit into the familiar and the comfortable, there is a greater chance that risks will be taken.

Modern learning theorists have found learning to be dependent upon active participation, reinforcement, feedback, variety, comprehension, and perceived relevance. [18] Although our educational system does not always make provision for such things, creative dramatics offers one way of developing some of these essentials. Using creative drama does not call for an overhaul of the entire educational system, and therein lies its best chance for future development. Creative drama offers to the teacher approaches that, using the materials and the environments already present, may engage students in experiences which prepare them for a world that is changing so rapidly that no one is certain what tomorrow may hold. Alvin Toffler in *Future Shock* makes a strong case for grounding all students in certain common skills needed for human communication and social integration; these skills would come under the headings of learning, relating, and choosing. He claims that if the pace of life continues at its present rate of acceleration, we shall have to anticipate increasing difficulty in making and maintaining meaningful human relationships. Educators who are concerned with the future of youths "must systematically organize formal and informal activities that help the student define, explicate, and test his values, whatever they are."[19] The curriculum of the future, then, calls for a combination of factual knowledge and training in what Toffler calls "life know-how." Somehow we must find ways to balance the two, developing environments which stimulate the production of both.

Children's drama holds a key in this process, but its acceptance as a valid part of the educational program will require some changes. Teachers will have to be educated as to its uses, for many individuals feel uneasy about launching into an area that requires as much personal involvement as does creative drama. We shall also have to think about the learning environment; the conventional box classroom, reminiscent of sterile prison cells, gradually must give way to more flexible environments. Already open classrooms are appearing: school architects are showing increased interest in spatial relationships and learning, and taxpayers are eager for ways to get the maximum education for the least money. With creative drama, the addition of greater space, movable furniture, different platform levels, and other equipment would make a difference;[20] but creative drama can operate without these things, and teachers should not rely on excuses of physical limitations to avoid becoming involved with drama.

All that is needed to make a beginning are imagination, a desire to engage students in activities which will begin to prepare them for life roles, and a teacher who feels that education should be an exciting, participatory experience that allows students to discover, to test, and to grow without fear.

Creative dramatics will not become the panacea for the many ills in our American educational system; but it does offer one way in which we can foster in our young people the creativity so vital for the continued development of a strong, democratic society.

Notes

1. Huxley, "Education on the Non-Verbal Level," p. 51.
2. Abt, "Education Is Child's Play," p. 128.
3. Rugg and Shumaker, *The Child-Centered School,* p. 264.
4. Coggin, *Uses of Drama,* pp. 292-93. Copyright © 1956 by George Braziller, Inc. Reprinted with the permission of the publisher.
5. See Duke, "Creative Dramatics: A Natural for the Multiple Elective Program."
6. Siks, "Introduction," in *Children's Theatre and Creative Dramatics,* ed. Siks and Dunnington, p. 5
7. Heathcote, "Drama," p. 138.
8. Muller, *The Uses of English,* p. 129.
9. Squire and Applebee, *Teaching English in the United Kingdom,* p. 198.

10. Squire and Applebee, *High School English Instruction Today.*
11. Squire and Applebee, *Teaching English in the United Kingdom,* p. 199.
12. Ibid., p. 197.
13. Moffett, *A Student-Centered Language Arts Curriculum,* p. 283.
14. Abt, "Education Is Child's Play," p. 123.
15. Squire and Applebee, *Teaching English in the United Kingdom,* p. 210.
16. Huxley, "Education on the Non-Verbal Level," p. 46.
17. George I. Brown, *Human Teaching for Human Learning,* p. 234.
18. Abt, "Education Is Child's Play," p. 123.
19. Toffler, *Future Shock,* pp. 355-59.
20. For a description of one British program utilizing some of these items, see Squire and Applebee, *Teaching English in the United Kingdom,* pp. 207-08. See also Yates, "Choose Your Environment."

PART TWO

Teaching
Creative Dramatics

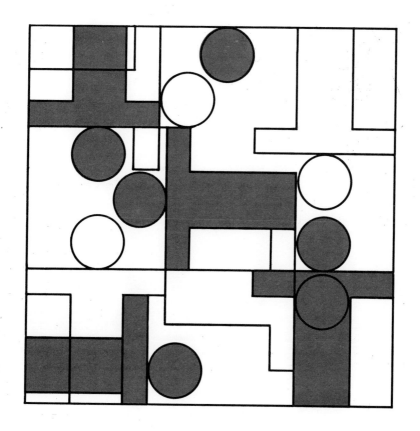

6 Creative Expression, Drama, and the Teacher

Those individuals who succeed in their chosen fields and who are happy while doing it have a basic outlook in common: they usually possess a friendly and sincere attitude toward humanity and a creative attitude toward their work, for they see in what they are doing an opportunity to enrich themselves in a creative fashion while helping others to achieve their goals.

Such a philosophy is basic to successful teaching. A great deal is said about the need for modern facilities, new methods, better texts, and other items for fostering educational growth in students. One cannot deny that such things are important, but undue emphasis upon them ignores the necessary aspects of creative teachers and teaching. What a teacher is and what his or her background has been often count more in determining success or failure as a creative teacher than any possible combination of teaching conditions, favorable or unfavorable.

Competent and creative teachers recognize that education should not bypass opportunities to release and facilitate creativity; in fact, such opportunities should be sought out and developed if they appear to be lacking within the existing educational framework. Naturally, teaching specific techniques or skills takes far less time in many instances than letting children work out problems for themselves; and within the modern system of education one often feels the push to cover a certain amount of material in a given time. For some reason we have come to equate covering material with developing knowledge, forgetting the side-effects which may develop along the way.

Many teachers have insisted that it is more economical to teach by authority. It seems, however, that many important things, though not all, can be learned more effectively and economically in creative ways

65

manifested by the students rather than because of authoritarian pressures from the teacher. It also appears that a number of people have especially strong preferences and aptitudes for learning creatively; that is, they learn more if freed to use their abilities in a creative way and, in contrast, they make remarkably little educational progress when teachers assume exclusive control over the way they are to learn.[1]

The truly creative teacher recognizes, therefore, that authoritarian emphasis and pressure can stifle creative expression and may lead to learning and personality problems if introduced at the wrong moment. To offset such practices, creative teaching offers "sensitive, insightful, developmental guidance which makes learning experiences optimally educative and conducive to the development and fulfillment of the creative personalities of individuals and groups."[2] Creative leadership also fosters opportunities to experience constructive social living and develops the kind of interaction which is responsive to shared values and common concerns.[3]

Obviously, then, creative education does not process learners into submissive conformists, but neither does it leave them at the mercy of their own impulses. Creative teaching is frequently misconstrued by educators as being total abdication of authority—a kind of "letting everyone do his own thing." Results from such an approach are inevitably chaotic and frequently damaging to both teacher and students. What creative teaching does mean is that on the part of both teacher and students the basic habit of independent thinking is encouraged and developed; for if a teacher is a mere conformist without a real thought of his own, he will never be successful in helping children to be independent themselves. Nor can he very well develop creative thinkers if he is not able to accept ideas and interpretations that differ radically from his own. One of the most important teaching skills needed in nurturing creative talents is the recognition and acknowledgment of potentialities, but this skill is difficult to obtain because acknowledging the potentiality of someone else is somehow threatening to the individual.[4] Still, those who wish to work with children must not only believe in them and in the values that come from keeping alive a child's creative spirit, but they must also accept the responsibility for guiding the child into channeling his energies toward dynamic and creative learning experiences.

The good teacher attempts to suggest only, and tries to recognize when something new is being added. He needs to know his students and what he can expect from them. When something different from his own conception appears, he recognizes it as such and adjusts accordingly. Sometimes a child may just be starting to use his imagination and any interruption at that point would kill the flow of confidence and ideas; educationally what is most difficult to bring forth from a child would be crushed.

Principles of Creative Teaching

Perhaps a consideration of the basic principles of general creative leadership could center around the following ideas. First is the need for imagination; without this, the teacher has little hope of becoming a creative individual, for the creative leader must find imaginative ways to awaken the magic of creation in others. He recognizes beauty in simplicity and is attuned to the richness of his surroundings; he makes use of the resources which are at hand and constantly strengthens his own imagination by using them.[5] The creative teacher instructs by example. He enters into the children's fun and learning with genuine enjoyment. Such a teacher will have the artist's approach to guiding, seizing the moment and bringing it into the realm of esthetic experience rather than allowing it to remain too long as a mere activity or exercise.[6] But creativity also demands a form of discipline. Children prefer a sense of order to formlessness, and the creative leader looks for ways to generate this order without inhibiting creative activity.[7] Along with this creative discipline goes a need to understand the basic laws of human nature and to apply them in treating each individual as a unique being. The teacher attempts to determine the specific needs and interests of every child, particularly those who seem difficult to understand. But above all, the creative teacher has a sound personal philosophy which allows him to be flexible and to accept the fact that frequently one has to make a hundred attempts in order to get a mere half-dozen good reactions.

An important adjunct to the creative teacher is the climate within the classroom. Unless teachers believe that young children can learn a great deal more in a rich environment and that frequently they accomplish more on their own, the educational process inevitably will stall. A cold, impersonal human environment blocks creative learning, as does a highly structured one in which a daily schedule is followed so tightly that no allowance can be made for spontaneity. Creative expression needs to be cultivated in a warmly human climate in which regimented routines do not take priority over human values.

How does a teacher develop such an environment? He can begin by making certain that he rewards creative behavior. E. Paul Torrance recommends three general ways by which a teacher can help students become aware that he wants them to be creative. Torrance suggests (1) that the teacher be respectful of unusual questions; this does not mean that all questions must be treated equally, but the teacher should train himself to see the potentialities within a student's questions as well as perhaps the desire for further exploration on the part of the student; (2) that in the same way, the teacher carefully consider imaginative and unusual ideas and treat them on their merits; using students' ideas is another way of showing them that what they think is of value; (3) that the teacher occasionally have students do things without the idea of evaluation, a kind of practice run where accuracy is not always the sole criterion.[8]

A representative creative environment, then, recognizes individual differences and encourages students to progress at their own paces. The teacher frees himself to permit varying approaches to the subject matter and allows students to work with a problem and to try different resources and reach tentative conclusions on their own. The need for knowing only one right answer—the one the teacher says is right—is distinctly de-emphasized, and punitive measures are avoided when incorrect responses appear. Instead, a mutual evaluation between teacher and student takes place, and new approaches are sketched for yet another and perhaps more successful attempt. Within this kind of climate the development of learning should be pleasant and meaningful for both students and teacher, and the result is bound to be a far more stable adjustment to the needs of social living.

The teacher who has the fine sensitivity and emotional maturity implied above can do much in this kind of atmosphere to help children with their social as well as academic adjustments. Creative dramatics is one approach which appears to work well in this kind of environment, much of its value coming from students and teacher living together daily in a situation where creating new and unusual ideas is standard.

But it must be pointed out that teaching drama is an intensely individual business. The teacher's approach to creative dramatics is bound to depend on his attitude toward discipline. If the teacher angers easily, cannot accept criticism, blows up if things go awry, demands immediate results or doesn't have the patience to let people move as rapidly or as slowly as they wish, and does not believe in introducing democratic procedures into the classroom, then he will not want to utilize creative dramatics in his teaching. Nothing is so good for children as a good dramatic experience—and nothing is so bad as a bad one. Undoubtedly the extremes of possibilities here are partly responsible for the insecurity which some people feel regarding dramatic work. Dorothy Heathcote, who in England has done extensive work with varying age groups in creative dramatics, offers the following important "thresholds" for the teacher to consider:

1. *Noise threshold*—What quality and quantity of noise first cause discomfort to the teacher?
2. *Space threshold*—What is the distance which the teacher feels must be maintained between himself and his class?
3. *Group-size threshold*—What sizes of groups are most comfortably handled by the teacher?
4. *Decision threshold*—In what ways are decisions made in teaching situations?[9]

If a teacher can tolerate a good deal of noise and, more important, allow the time to make the drama feasible, then he may discover that creative dramatics will open new ways to touch upon the creative spirits of his students. Of course, certain skills are involved in understanding how to use drama for creative purposes. The teacher needs to acquire an understanding of dramatic elements and how they combine—sometimes contrasting, sometimes supporting each other—to make meaningful statements. A vivid pictorial and aural imagination is helpful, as is an empathy for the general mood of the group. The capacity to put children's needs ahead of the teacher's is understood; hence flexibility in the teaching role becomes vital. The teacher must also be able to deal with subtle changes of register in verbal communication; and, finally, he must possess the ability to look—to perceive the real situation in its full dimensions.[10]

The extent to which a teacher will take an active part in creative activity must depend, once more, on the kind of person he is. An example can stimulate but it can also inhibit. To break down the resistance which often occurs toward something new, the teacher may wish to demonstrate, even if it is only to show that he is not afraid of making a fool of himself occasionally—humility in teaching can be an asset at times. Most outstanding drama teachers operate as unobtrusively as possible, attempting by an occasional provocative question to lead students into more concentrated imaginative activity. This method sometimes seems to involve a great amount of "wasted time," but usually it is found that the time "wasted," as a skeptic is likely to put it, is actually well employed, for though there may be no immediate dramatic end-product, there is a cumulative liberation which paves the way for much more meaningful experiences next time.[11] It may happen, of course, that some teachers will desire a more controlled situation; this actually may be advisable, particularly if space is lacking. Occasionally, too, the justification can be made that not enough time is available for students to evolve their own discipline; and then, as we have mentioned, not all teachers are suited to the completely free approach. But even the presence of some restrictions does not mean that dramatic activity of a worthwhile nature cannot occur.

No matter what approach he takes in using creative dramatics in the classroom, the teacher will find himself playing many roles. At times it may be necessary for him to oppose the common view of the situation deliberately in order to suggest options and to aid clarity of thought. On other occasions a narrator will be needed to help set the mood and to register the various events as they occur. Sometimes the teacher becomes a suggester of ideas, but only as a member of the group. Students who assume lead roles may need support as they explore yet unknown boundaries of leadership. The teacher may have to arbitrate when disagreements arise over methods of playing, choices of materials, and division of roles. And, too, it may prove helpful at times to adopt the role of the "obtuse" one who requires to be shown, to be informed, and who believes that only the students can do it.[12]

Teacher Training in Creative Dramatics

With all these responsibilities, the question often arises as to whether the classroom teacher is fully capable of using creative dramatics effectively or whether it might be better to have someone who has been specially trained in the field. Comments from various classroom teachers indicate a need for better understanding on this point. For instance, one teacher says, "Creative dramatics is a luxury. I can't afford time for it . . . where children need to learn so many skills."[13] Another teacher puts it this way:

> It's a pretty tough world children are growing up in and the question in my mind is whether we should concentrate on arming them with as much realism and subject matter as possible or soften it up for them with a goodly portion of sensitive, sweet, creative ideas in dramatic situations. I don't think children should escape realism when they are young. Why build up their egos and have them shattered later? And shattered they will be unless they know exactly who they are and what they are.[14]

The attitudes of both teachers involve misunderstandings in need of correction. Obviously neither of them knows much about the role of creative dramatics in education. In cases such as these the teacher undoubtedly would do more harm than good if he engaged his students in creative drama activities. Unless a teacher understands the various roles of drama he cannot understand how creative dramatics integrates with living and learning. Creative dramatics is not something soft or separate from life. As art, it is an attempt to integrate and enrich life, not to escape from reality.

But a division of opinion exists about placing creative drama specialists in the schools. During the early 1900s when creative dramatics was beginning to appear in the schools as a result of the work of Winifred Ward and others, the controversy became quite heated. John Merrill, who taught drama at the Francis W. Parker School in Chicago, claimed that "only a trained teacher, conversant with the laws of the art of dramatic expression, can understand and guide the student as he makes his way through the melodramatic period of development into the realistic realm and finally approaches the desired period of suggestion and real artistry of expression."[15] On the other hand, Frances Presler, who was a supervisor of creative activities in the Winnetka, Illinois, schools at about the same time, said, "It does not matter where the teacher teaches or how untrained she may be. If she loves children sincerely, is sensitive to their feelings, is willing to steep herself with the children in a rich background, and work for honesty of expression, and to wait for natural child growth, then the joy of creative dramatics may be hers." [16] Actually both positions are reconcilable, although Merrill tended to favor the formal aspects of drama.

A good leader, specialist or not, knows and enjoys drama from having experienced it. It is absurd to say that no teacher needs preparation for doing drama, but it is equally ridiculous to maintain that a teacher who sees the values of using drama in education needs a course in formal theater. All teachers, if possible, should have some practical experience in creative dramatic work, partly to enable them to teach it but equally as important to help their own self-development. Enjoyment in dramatic work means enthusiasm about sharing it with children. One teacher who took part in a creative dramatics workshop and who was experimenting with rhythm for the first time said, "It was important to me that I played that bell just in the unique way that I felt it. It was part of me. And I suddenly realized that I had to be there to play. Everyone else was depending on me in that group. It must be the same way for the child." [17] This person will undoubtedly become a better teacher of dramatic activity because she has experienced some of the feelings which her own students need to have.

The training available for teachers, however, is limited. Anthony Adams, an Englishman, has urged the teaching profession in England to ask for such training.

> We would urge upon training institutions the need to give teachers experience in drama work as part of their professional training, in practice rather than simply in theory; and we would see the English department of the school as an important instrument of training here. It is possible, for example, to combine classes so that the teacher with the most experience in drama can work alongside his less expert colleagues and in this way can help their training while educating the children also. A particular value of drama lies in its flexibility which adapts it to both group and team teaching methods. [18]

Adams' concern and his suggestion are equally important in the United States, where far too little has been done in the way of training.

Some progress has been made, but the majority of teachers in America, particularly those in secondary schools, have had no exposure to drama other than perhaps one or two survey courses; their knowledge about creative drama in particular is negligible, if existent at all. It is therefore no surprise that creative dramatics as part of an individual's teaching strategies appears only infrequently in American classrooms. Some colleges and universities, nevertheless, are making attempts to encourage students to take some courses in creative drama.

The University of Washington, for example, has rather extensive course offerings in children's drama. They include the following:

Children's Theater: children's theater direction and laboratory work

Creative Dramatics: beginning and advanced courses and laboratory; practice teaching, special projects, and seminars

Introduction to Children's Drama: includes children's theater, creative dramatics, and puppetry (required of all drama majors)

Puppetry: beginning and advanced courses and productions

Other: creative dramatics demonstration classes offered; five age groups from age 5 through senior high led by faculty; 8 observations required. One major production a year; 12 to 14 performances as well as additional Master's thesis productions. Basic field of learning in children's drama offered elementary education majors (40 hours in drama). B.A. and M.A. degrees in drama with emphasis in children's drama offered.

Very few other colleges or universities have programs so extensive as this one.[19] However, there is no reason why inservice institutes offering lectures and discussions on the basic philosophy and technique could not be offered. Participation in actual playmaking can help teachers throw off some of their own adult inhibitions and can offer them opportunities to rediscover the powers of the imagination. Then too, reading the literature in the field of creative drama and the creative process helps to bring new insight and appreciation to the teaching of classroom drama. Reading and analyzing plays, stories, and poems suitable for dramatization offers additional practical help. Observations of children's groups in action shows how the theories learned are actually put into practice. All that is needed for such inservice courses is a demand for them from teachers and willing and trained personnel from a university's theater or education department.[20]

If such inservice courses are not feasible because of location or other difficulties, perhaps a one-day workshop in creativity would offer teachers some help in preparing for the use of creative dramatics. Some teachers have immersed themselves in encounter groups or sensitivity training where members learn to ventilate their emotions. The greatest difficulty here is the negativism which often thrives in such groups when leadership does not always function adequately. An alternative would be a more gradual process, moving from relatively comfortable experiences to those which involve taking greater risks.

George I. Brown outlines a possible workshop which would follow such an arrangement. He suggests that group members first meet together and discuss the idea of creativity, using examples from the current literature about what constitutes the creative as opposed to the non-creative personality. Then members would be asked to engage in three kinds of activity; the first would be a completely verbal activity such as trying to describe an object; the second would be a combined verbal and body activity; and the third would be essentially nonverbal. He suggests using the brainstorming technique—members respond spontaneously to questions such as "What if you were made smaller, how would you feel?" For the second activity members might use a type of charades with speech—for example, portraying a mound of ice cream from the point of view of an ant; and finally, for the nonverbal, members engage in some aspect of pantomime.[21]

The next step would be to use a form of synectics developed by William J. J. Gordon which employs three levels of analogical thinking.

A. *Direct analogy*—an object is examined, and from what it looks like or what it reminds one of the individual is asked to come up with names of other objects, no matter how obscurely related—in fact, the more obscurely related the better. Spontaneity is encouraged. Participants are urged to stop thinking too hard and let the ideas come through naturally.

B. *Symbolic analogy*—the same or another object is used and participants are asked what its characteristics remind them of. What is its essence or symbolic meaning, and what other objects can this symbolic meaning be assigned to?

C. *Personal analogy*—the participants are asked to focus on an object and through intense concentration actually to become the object. How do you feel? What object comes to mind as you experience this feeling?[22]

These activities, which have grown progressively more personal, are followed by participating in "another universe." Paintings—realistic, impressionistic, or abstract—are displayed around the room. The group is asked to select one picture to which all the members of the group will respond. Then they are given the following instructions: "As you look at the picture, enter it; you may become one of the persons or one of the objects in the picture; or you may stay yourself, but walk right in. Talk about how you feel while you are there." And then, finally, each person is asked to make a road map of his life. He may start from birth and trace his life to the present, or he may begin in the present and paint his future as he anticipates it. Each person then talks through his road map and explains it to others.

Although these experiences may seem a far cry from academic training in creative drama, some basic similarities do exist. Both kinds of training call for an examination of the self and a developing awareness of others; both call for a heightening of the imaginative powers and their application to various problems. The function of such training is to help the individual experience what he really is. Such awareness training teaches one to listen and to see who is there. Too often teachers "see" a concept of an individual student which is not really true of the child as he exists at the moment; subsequent learning experiences based on the teacher's concept of the child may have little relevance for that student. And as we consider the role of creativity and creative dramatics in teaching, being aware of the student as he really is completes half the battle toward more effective teaching and learning.

Parents, too, often wish to become involved in creative drama. The Free Library of Philadelphia, Pennsylvania, offers workshops for adults who are interested in guiding children through initial creative drama experiences. The workshops meet for fifteen weeks and during that time explore the essentials of action, plot, character, and dialogue. The participants also gain practical guidance and experience in selecting, sharing, and using a variety of library materials as beginnings for dramatization and improvisations.[23]

It should be evident that some practice as well as good creative imagination helps to teach playmaking. Many teachers have experimented but have not known how much to expect from children. Most have not begun simply enough and have expected too much too soon. Even though the teacher may encourage students to use their own initiative, he still has to know how to help them see the possibilities in a situation. Brian Way in *Development through Drama* makes this point clearly.

> It is important to remember that in the early stages of all creative work the participants experience a kind of fear of freedom, which can be a total uncertainty as to what to do; ideas either don't come or are self-rejected as inadequate; there is need for someone to give a start. In the realm of ideas on what to do and, later on, who to be, each member of the class is fully dependent for all the beginning stages.[24]

Therefore, the questions to ask and the ideas to throw into the discussions can be vital to the development of creative activity. Because of this some of the best work with children in creative dramatics is done by the classroom teacher who really understands what the children are doing; yet strangely enough, a teacher may have little formal knowledge of drama and still make the process work. Perhaps appreciation and discriminating taste combined with the power of intelligent observation are far more important.

Children profit from the attention of both the classroom teacher and the creative dramatics specialist. The classroom teacher is in an excellent position to guide indirectly; he knows his students and can capitalize on moments of spontaneous activity and encourage individual expression. He is also able to utilize time effectively by developing creative learning experiences and through these integrate subject matter.[25]

The special teacher of creative dramatics usually has a greater background in drama and can bring fresh ideas and experiences to the children and the classroom teacher. It is probably in the best interests of both students and teacher that the drama specialist not take over the children's activities completely but work instead with classroom teachers to train them in the art of creative dramatics. Drama is a central part of the learning experience, not an extra or a minor speciality.[26]

The teacher faces an important challenge in determining how he chooses to utilize drama in the classroom. For success he must consider how to create an appropriate climate where value judgments are not final and where honesty and individuality are treasured. He must be willing to employ children's ideas and make them work positively within a world where the child's concepts and values coexist with those of the adult world. He also must be aware of the ways in which drama may function in promoting the release of varying and conflicting attitudes within the group; and, most importantly, he must be able to move the work toward teaching ends without destroying the children's contributions or sense of involvement.

The art of creative dramatics demands a dedication of one's energies and talents, but the teacher—specialist or not—who truly cares for children and believes in the beauty of drama and self-expression will find ways for sharing creative dramatics with his students, and in the process he will be opening the way for new and meaningful learning experiences.

Notes

1. Torrance, *Encouraging Creativity in the Classroom,* p. 1.
2. Zirbes, *Spurs to Creative Teaching,* p. 36.
3. Ibid., p. 24.
4. Torrance, "Nurture of Creative Talents," p. 189.
5. Siks, *Creative Dramatics,* pp. 122-24.
6. Ibid., p. 128.
7. Ibid., pp. 142-43.
8. Torrance, *Rewarding Creative Behavior,* p. 43.
9. Heathcote, "How Does Drama Serve Thinking, Talking, and Writing?" p. 1080.
10. Heathcote, "Drama," p. 144.
11. Creber, *Sense and Sensitivity,* p. 86.
12. Heathcote, "Drama," pp. 144-45.
13. Siks, *Creative Dramatics,* p. 120.
14. Ibid., pp. 12-21.
15. Merrill, "Dramatics: A Mode of Study," p. 70.
16. Presler, "Developing Dramatics in the Public Schools," p. 46.
17. Gillies, "We Believe," p. 71.
18. Cited in Barnes, ed., *Drama in the English Classroom,* p. 50.
19. See *Directory of American Colleges and Universities Offering Training in Children's Theatre and Creative Dramatics,* rev. ed., for other colleges and universities' offerings in children's drama. See also Haaga, "Recommended

Training for Creative Dramatics Leaders," and Appendixes A and B of this book.

20. This type of inservice course has been run with success. See Kase, "Theatre Resources for Youth in New Hampshire."
21. George I. Brown, "Teaching Creativity to Teachers and Others."
22. Gordon, *Synectics.* See George I. Brown, *Human Teaching for Human Learning,* p. 42, for another explanation of this process.
23. Fertik, "A Crescendo: Creative Dramatics in Philadelphia."
24. Way, *Development through Drama,* p. 26.
25. See George I. Brown, *Human Teaching for Human Learning,* pp. 53-192, for various examples of how this integration occurs.
26. Moffett, *A Student-Centered Language Arts Curriculum,* pp. 283-84.

Dramatic activities transcend the traditional but largely artificial boundaries of school subjects, fusing them into a unified and significant whole. The broader sympathy and the wider knowledge of one's fellows which dramatic activity inculcates enrich understanding.

Government of Northern Ireland Ministry of Education, *Provision for Primary Schools,* p. 34

7 A Sequence and Suggested Methods for Guiding Children in Creative Dramatics

When creative dramatics is a part of an integrated educational program, it can add meaning and richness to almost every aspect of educational activity. Strong impressions demand strong expression; and if in social studies, literature, and other subject areas students are exposed to thoughts, ideas, and emotions, they should have the opportunities to react to them in creative and constructive ways. For this reason the use of the dramatic approach in teaching subject matter as well as social relationships should be considered by all educators.

To assure that experiences in drama will be meaningful, however, the educator must keep certain principles in mind as he looks for different ways to utilize creative drama in his subject field. One is that the audience-performer relationship, normally found in regular drama, is to be kept to a minimum as much as possible. When the entire classroom is used and not just the front areas, students think less of performance and become used to new spatial relationships, an important part of freeing self-expression. Initial activities should be class-oriented, with all students participating at the same time whenever possible. Eventually some students may become observers and some actors, but with the roles being exchanged frequently. When adverse reactions to observation are overcome, the teacher can take this as a signal to move on to more involved and individualized activity. The best order of activities, then, is class, group, and finally individual.

But just being aware of the sequence of activities is not enough. If the teacher wishes to see his efforts bring meaningful results, he has some preliminary work to do. One of the most important considerations is the students with whom he will be working. What are their needs? Should the emphasis be placed on group activities or individual ones? Is there a need to break down social-emotional barriers and get involved in action, or is there perhaps a greater need for sitting and expressing through discussion? What is the composition of the group—proportions of boys and girls, ethnic groups represented? And then there are the questions about experiential background. What are the present experiences of the class? How much linguistic and experiential background do the students have for the activity in mind? Should some kinds of experiences be built before going to the actual drama? Does the class respond readily to emotional appeal? What in general are its emotional reactions?

The answers to these questions will vary widely from class to class, but the answers are important, for they dictate in large measure how one approaches creative drama with students. For instance, with students who are quite immature, the teacher will wish to spend considerable time on preliminary activities that will build their confidence and success. Direct work with the emotions probably should be postponed for a time until students demonstrate their ability and willingness to involve themselves in such activity. Work with movement, certain types of pantomime, and then improvisation will usually bring the best results.

But consideration of background is important as well. Students find it very difficult to play convincingly in experiences which have little connection to their own backgrounds. In cases where the lack of experiential background is pronounced, the teacher may wish to begin close to his students' present resources and then gradually introduce materials and ideas which help them expand beyond their present states.

Adolescents tend to be very conscious of each other, and some difficulty may be experienced when working with a mixed group. Activities should be carefully structured to avoid highlighting differences between sexes or ethnic groups. In most instances, however, if the teacher follows the general principle of working with the entire class first, then working with smaller selected groups, and finally introducing individual activities, these problems will be alleviated.

One of the essential ingredients for success in the creative dramatics program lies in the choice of materials and activities. Initially these should have clear action and lend themselves to a simple sequence of development which moves toward a climax, whether it be in work with sound or in story creation. For this reason teachers often find it easier to begin with a well-chosen story than to attempt to use materials created entirely spontaneously. It will be necessary to develop certain skills of concentration and focus, however, before undertaking complex materials; so it is recommended that in most cases students be taken through a sequential development of activities. For some students the order of treating the various aspects of creative dramatics is not too important; but individuals who are just beginning—and this frequently is the case on the secondary level—usually profit from spending time on activities which insure some sense of continuity and increasing complexity.

Rhythm and Movement

One of the first steps toward a sequential development of skills in creative drama comes through work with rhythm and movement. A principal function of movement in drama is to help the young person achieve complete mastery of his or her physical self. Adolescents in particular are very conscious of their bodies and tend to view themselves as uncoordinated and ugly. It is important to develop an emotional harmony in the student regarding his or her body and abilities, and this can be done only by helping the student develop personal confidence and sensitivity.[1]

The teacher must be aware, however, of his own attitudes toward movement. If the teacher feels uncomfortable, students will too; he should not practice at the expense of students nor push beyond his own limits of comfort and competence. But the teacher must be willing to explore and develop on his own and should, if necessary, do some preliminary work for his own peace of mind before engaging his students in movement activity. Patrick Creber points out that free movement work is important to the development of the child, particularly the one who does not verbalize easily.

> Therapeutic value of free movement work is immeasurably greater because it involves more of the whole personality in a way writing cannot. Writing as a means of fantasy-expression is in any case confined by words, or by the lack of them; obviously many of those who have the greatest need of free expression in writing are precisely those whose level of intelligence is below average and who . . . have the poorest verbal equipment to start with. Theoretically, in free drama everyone is equal, though of course some more so than others; but, at least, virtually all have the same basic equipment.[2]

Sometimes, then, the work in movement serves as a stimulus for creation in other media and enables the child to overcome certain deficiencies in skills such as writing. Hence simple exercises in movement may allow the student to experience success in areas where he has failed before. For example, Terry Borton, working with children in the schools of Philadelphia, has found that their creativity is often released through simple movement experiences. He asks pairs of students to lock the fingers of their right hands together so that the thumbs are upright and free, as in the old game of thumbfighting; then students are to imagine that they are their thumbs and that their thumbs must meet. Students work with this experience for a time and then are asked to write, if they wish, haiku or very short poems about their experiences in this exercise. Here are some of the results:

Second grade

> We played together
> We looked eye to eye
> He said hi to me.

Fifth grade

> We had a wild fight
> and we trapped each other down
> till we got tired.

College level

> The fat scrunchy thumbs
> hide, hello, hit, hug and hurt
> just like little me's.[3]

In most beginning sessions with movement, though, the teacher will usually introduce a single idea or mood. Students are asked to respond to that idea or mood, sometimes with music providing a background for the activity. We often forget the possible uses of music; in learning, music stimulates a response and helps to build a certain environment in which a student feels motivated to move and explore space. The relationship between music and movement as it applies to young people is important, because young people do not as a rule make or enjoy the conscious intellectual analysis of musical form in any detail.[4] Brian Way claims that "if the language of music is too complicated, then the child is unable to do anything in response to it; if it is clear, and its clarity lies in its time-beat and rhythm, then its message is easily understood and acted upon."[5] Children at an early age delight in a straightforward time beat and only gradually come to discover and enjoy the use of rhythm, whether offered in a straight time beat or in one with consistent changes of emphasis. Adults, of course, tend to reject pop music because of its very clear time beat, and often they make the mistake of trying to substitute "good music" while students are attempting introductory work in movement. A gradual introduction to more complex music should be the general rule, for, as the child develops, a refinement of rhythmic perception and action will start to appear in his life.

Consequently one proceeds with caution when using recorded music. Class members will tend to follow the music; and although this does offer a form of discipline and suggests form and structure, it is advisable to use recordings sparingly at first because students may not be able to carry a structure suggested by the music for very long. Simple improvised rhythms created by using the hands or some object such as a ruler tapping on the edge of a desk often work just as effectively (see additional suggestions about creating rhythmic patterns in part three, "Handbook of Resources"). However, a child cannot be entirely freed just with outer imposed rhythms. Emotions control the deep muscles within us that govern our breath and bodies. A child's body becomes free only when faith and confidence are given to him emotionally.[6]

Rhythmic and bodily movement exercises call for a variety of activities, including imitation of things in nature—flowers, animals; reaction to emotions—joy, sadness, fear; as well as imaginative responses to pronounced rhythms. The emphasis is always on adaptability, and the student learns to be flexible by changing his actions as his mood and the environment change. Something similar to the following activity may evolve after children have been working with movement for a time. This observation occurred at a British school where ten year olds were working with music.

> Teacher: "Face the wall." All children turn outwards to the wall in a circle around the room.
>
> Teacher: "Listen to the music." They listen to the improvised piano music.
>
> Teacher: "Burglars walking on tiptoe." They become burglars. (Music stealthy).
>
> Teacher: "Carrying heavy bags." (Sudden change to slow music with pronounced beat).
>
> Teacher: "Now you are a forest, all standing about." (Music stops abruptly). They take up an attitude of trees, quite still with arms and hands in weird positions.
>
> Teacher: "Wind starts blowing. Here it comes." (Dramatic scale from bass on piano, ending in sudden climax chord). All fall down and remain quiet and relaxed.[7]

Success such as this does not appear immediately, and certain modifications will be necessary to meet age levels and space requirements. But the essential ingredients of imaginative response and flexibility are integral to any movement work. Rhythm and movement never completely disappear from dramatics, for drama is based on action, and no matter whether the student does a free exercise or a scripted play, he will find himself calling upon both rhythm and movement to express himself.

As can be seen in the British example, a considerable diversification of sound may occur, and this is important for the development of perceptual discrimination, emotional range, and bodily articulation. Shifting the stress in rhythm, speeding up and slowing down, raising and lowering or shortening and lengthening notes offer wide latitude for response from students and increase the degree of creative invention. Running the sound spectrum is actually running the gamut of emotion, and learning to discriminate various auditory dynamics helps sensitize students to pattern and structure in other media, including literature.[8]

Though movement to sound and rhythm may not at first glance seem directly related to the development of speech, it does lay an important base. For the small child, speech is only one physical activity among many. For him speech accompanies other actions and justifies itself only when it can do what other actions cannot. Movement to sound and rhythm permits the child to develop his powers of nonverbal expression and also allows him to experience their limitations.[9]

Kinesics and Space

But body movement is important in other ways as well. Certain aspects of body movement have become a matter of scientific investigation in the field of kinesics, which is the systematic examination of nonlingual body motion in its relation to communication.[10] The average person is little aware of how body motion influences communication. As adults we have learned to move in conjunction with our minds and our tongues, and we seldom stop to consider that body movement is really a vital means of expression. Take, for example, the way space influences behavior. Since none of us has probably been taught to look at space as isolated from other associations, actual feelings which are prompted by the handling of space are usually attributed to some other source. Yet in growing up, people learn literally thousands of spatial cues, all of which have their own meaning in their own context. For example, it does not take long for students to become aware of the distribution of space in a classroom. Each student has his desk area which he comes to regard as his own; on occasion he even will fight to protect it. Just as apparent is the area belonging to the teacher, normally located in the front of the classroom and including a desk and perhaps a blackboard. A student approaching this area may have a sense of entering a foreign territory. He may not necessarily attribute the feeling to any awareness of spatial rights, but indirectly this is what takes place, for mankind has developed his territorial sense to an almost unbelievable extent.

Still, we tend to treat space somewhat in the same fashion as sex: it's there but we don't talk about it openly. For some unknown reason our culture has told us to play down or repress the feelings we may have about space. Watch, for example, when someone comes into a person's living room for the first time. More often than not the visitor will select the chair that the host has just vacated; then, for some reason, the visitor will sense that this was his host's chair and he will pop up, asking if the chair, indeed, had been the host's. In turn, the host will say quite quickly that it makes no difference; he can sit elsewhere. Nevertheless, in the background during all of this action, a vague sense of irritation rests with the host because his personal spatial territory has been invaded.

Although one would not wish to suggest that space and movement within it are totally reliable as means for evaluating an individual and his intentions, certain aspects of communication evaluation do seem to rely rather heavily on just such factors. Particularly important seems to be the handling of space during speech activity. Not only can a vocal message be qualified by the handling of distance, but the substance of a conversation can often demand special handling of spatial relationships. Edward Hall, a noted anthropologist, made an extensive study of this aspect of communication and discovered that one of the most highly elaborated forms of spatial interaction occurs during speech. Observing people in different countries, he noted that the way this interaction was handled varied from country to country. After careful experiments he was able to establish certain guidelines regarding distance and speech which Americans in particular seem to follow.

1. Very close (3 in. to 6 in.) — Soft whisper, top secret
2. Close (8 in. to 12 in.) — Audible whisper, very confidential
3. Near (12 in. to 20 in.) — Indoors, soft voice; outdoors, full voice, confidential
4. Neutral (20 in. to 36 in.) — Soft voice, low volume; personal subject matter
5. Neutral (4½ ft. to 5ft.) — Full voice; information of non-personal matter
6. Public distance (5½ ft. to 8 ft.) — Full voice with slight over-loudness; public information for others
7. Across the room (8 ft. to 20 ft.) — Loud voice; talking to a group
8. Stretching the limits of distance — 20 ft. to 24 ft. indoors; up to 100 ft. outdoors; hailing distance, departure[11]

Frequently people violate these guidelines unconsciously and then are quite puzzled by the reactions they receive from others. When a person is traveling in a foreign country the reaction may be quite pronounced. In Latin America, for example, people like to remain very close to the person with whom they are speaking. Americans may find this closeness quite offensive and as a result may tend to back away from the speaker; the Latin American pursues, and one can imagine the resulting ludicrous scenes in which communication reaches an impasse.

Students need to be aware of these aspects of spatial relationships which affect communication, and the classroom provides a suitable environment for learning experiences. Work in movement and a conscious exploration of spatial relationships help to make an individual a more responsible and sensitive communicator. Being able to define space, adjust to territorial rights, and move with sensitivity to promote greater expression are attainable goals.

Although it may appear that some work in creative drama is done in isolation, it is nevertheless essential to a sense of development for the students that these skills be carried over to subject fields and social situations. Once students have been introduced to various types of experiences in movement, for example, the teacher should then seek ways to utilize these developing skills in approaching subject assignments. The previously cited example of creative writing is just one such approach; others include movement interpretation of poetry, demonstrations of characteristic movements in other cultures, and even dance improvisation. In most instances, however, older students will need movement work only as warm-up and for establishing an appropriate climate; they will then move to other areas of work.

Mime and Pantomime

After students have become accustomed to responding to sound and rhythm, have had experience in defining spatial relationships, and seem to feel comfortable with such work, they are ready to move on to formal mime or pantomime. The latter often grows out of work in rhythm with little coaxing from the teacher, for the child feels the need to express himself in some kind of constructive movement. According to Kathrine Sorley Walker, mime is "the accomplishment of conveying sense without speech, by imitating action or by using gesture which someone else understands."[12] It is a common misconception, however, that pantomime is merely a way of doing without words; actually it is more like thinking overheard, for it begins and ends before words have formed themselves. Therefore pantomime is predominantly an art in which the mind is the master.[13] To children the art offers considerable pleasure because it combines the harmony of music, the rhythm of bodily movements and dance, and the persuasive powers of words by outward expression.[14]

Clowning and pantomime are sometimes considered to be synonymous; but a considerable amount of the buffoonery which occurs in clowning is not real mime in the sense of portraying feeling by expression. Some of the great clowns such as Emmett Kelley, Charlie Chaplin, and the renowned Oleg Popov of the U.S.S.R. could command a large audience even in the most simple scenes. A good illustration of this can be seen in the following description of Popov:

> He [Popov] wanders on, alone, into the great ring, finds a pool of golden glow from a spotlight, and as he looks up at it with joy,

unfastening his coat, it becomes the summer sun. He settles down, relaxes, opens a bag, and takes out a picnic—bread and cheese and a bottle of drink. Enjoying the warmth, he lies down, stretching out, his cap over his eyes, to sleep. The spotlight moves off him, and he wakes up cold, shivering, rubbing his hands, buttoning up his coat, and hunts around for the lost sunlight. He finds it on the other side of the ring and begins to relax, but it is fitful and starts to fade. Desperately he tries to scoop it up, to gather it, even a little of it, and stuff it into his bag, but it all slips away.[15]

No concerted attempt should be made to develop students into polished performers, but the emotions suggested in the above scene are well within reach of most students, once they have become relaxed enough to sense how they can reveal their emotions through bodily expression. It does not take students long to see that a distinct difference exists between the pantomime of a boy woodenly doing the dishes after supper and that of a boy washing the dishes while the ball team waits impatiently under the kitchen window. The latter has the tension and the conflict which constitute drama.

Pantomime obviously demonstrates that drama comes from within the individual; the pantomimist who does a good job is the one who through the power of movement is able to communicate his ideas and inner emotions to others. The use of the power of movement encourages the shy child to volunteer participation; he does not have to rely on direct verbalization but instead can use his body as a means of communication. Frequently from this kind of release the reticent child will find reason to speak and will be stimulated to increase his vocabulary.[16]

Mime, like many other aspects of creative drama, requires an initial period of physical stillness during which a subject is mentally explored, perhaps tentatively at first and then with growing emotional involvement and deepening focus and concentration.[17] Emphasis is placed on relaxing the mind and body; a good way to begin is by trying to empty students' minds of preoccupations (see part three, "Handbook of Resources," for suggestions). The deeper the initial physical and interior stillness, the greater the ultimate potential of the exercise. Regular practice in the right kind of relaxation helps to insure a receptive classroom climate; students soon realize that the relaxation and the emphasis upon concentration are merely a prelude for experiences which call for letting out natural energy. Mime enlarges the powers of the imagination; and imagination is the force that raises man to his highest level, either by making him create and appreciate or by making him sensitive to the needs and reactions of his fellowmen.[18]

With very young children the teacher may wish to begin work in pantomime by telling simple stories, acting out nursery rhymes and songs, or through individual interpretations of assorted rhythms. Older children can be led to see the different types of movement in pantomime. They may begin with action movements which are simply and solely those necessary to the performance of an act such as walking or running. Students then proceed to movements delineating character; these are more permanent and determine the type of character, his habits, and the quality of the impersonation. Following these are instinctive movements; spontaneous and involuntary, these actions portray emotion or a moral or a physical sensation. After this come descriptive or speaking movements. These are studied and constructed to express a certain thought, need, or wish. Finally, the well-schooled pantomimist graduates to complementary movements. These entail the cooperation of the entire body in conveying the meaning indicated by the chief movement so that the expression is given additional force and harmony.[19]

Pantomime is an essential step in the development of creative dramatics and the emerging expressiveness of the student. All sorts of actions, ranging from the simplest to the most complex, should be worked into the students' development. Even guessing games help stimulate creativity and improve the ability to judge inferences. Charades is probably the best known of these games, but the teacher can develop others as needs arise. Activities of this type make for a healthy development of audience-performer relationships as well as a fast feedback. The actor learns quickly whether he is communicating. Both audience and actor learn communicative precision; one by words, the other by gestures. The audience and actor must develop flexibility in interpretation and wording because alternatives have to be offered as well. The essential skill of the pantomimist is to play on association. Such a skill is invaluable in learning to communicate because one has to know what facts and concepts are shared and therefore can be counted on for communicating.[20]

Speech and mime are closely related; the proper expression of words calls for a vivid and imaginative conception of what one wishes to convey, and there is no better stimulant to the imagination than the practice of conveying ideas solely by visual means.

The use of pantomime suggests an area of speech which is sometimes overlooked. Occasionally referred to as "body English"—a popular synonym for certain aspects of kinesics—the uses of facial expression and bodily movement often have strong impact upon meaning and communication. A political figure gives a speech which is supposed to be reassuring, yet it has the opposite effect. Why? Simply because sentences cease to have meaning by themselves if other communicative signs become much more eloquent. Trite as it may sound, what people do frequently becomes more important than what they say. Gestures and other facets of body English serve as a reinforcement for meaning;

without them we are often at a loss as to the exact meaning being conveyed. Likewise, when body movements seem to contradict speech we are confused and the effectiveness of the communication is lost, for we can no longer effectively evaluate what we are hearing. In some aspects, nonverbal communication patterns are more important than verbal ones because the nonverbal patterns are unconscious—a person cannot so easily hide his real feelings in such a case. Research suggests that nonverbal patterns may differ from culture to culture. A good example of such differences in patterned communicative behavior is found in comparing the cultures of blacks and whites. Kenneth Johnson, in an article entitled "Black Kinesics—Some Non-Verbal Communication Patterns in the Black Culture," states that many black children are taught not to look an older person in the eye when the older person is talking to them. To do so would be to communicate disrespect. Johnson also notes that a "culture clash" can develop if people are ignorant of the meaning of the action. He says:

> . . . in the dominant culture, eye contact is interpreted one way, while it is interpreted in another way within the Black culture. Avoidance of eye contact by a Black person communicates, "I am in a subordinate role and I respect your authority over me," while the dominant cultural member may interpret avoidance of eye contact as "Here is a shifty, unreliable person I'm dealing with."[21]

Another interesting aspect of the shifts which these communicative patterns go through is illustrated by the differences in the uses of the "rapping stance." Originally rapping stance referred to a young black male's stance when he was talking romantically to a young black female; whites have adopted the term "rap" and now use it in reference to any type of aggressive talk on any subject; the stance may be somewhat similar to that of the black.[22] Students may be aware of such differences in a vague way but may not know how to go about correcting their own problems of bodily expression or their interpretation of others'. With some guided experiences in the classroom, though, most students become much more effective in the use of body English; this, in turn, makes them more alert to the movements of others.

Pantomime, then, is one of the most obvious ways to heighten awareness about communication. To begin associating pantomime activity with speech skill, some introduction to the language of classical ballet or other sign languages may be helpful (see pantomime section in the "Handbook of Resources"). Students might also study their own movements via playback on videotape. With frequent experiences in pantomime activity, a corresponding increase in sensitivity to the factors affecting communication should become apparent.

The only restrictions on pantomime are space and control. Often in scenes of conflict, a child, fearful of hurting his partner, will become self-conscious and break character.[23] Demonstration followed by evaluation can help students realize the importance of control and safety precautions. Quick movements, positions that limit the audience's view, and exaggerated motions all may suggest force without harm. Again, with practice and encouragement, students learn to adjust their bodies and actions to each other. It is an impressive sight to see thirty or forty youngsters moving rapidly in a fairly small space, having absolute control of their bodies, free to weave ingenious patterns, combinations, and characterizations.

Improvisation

Success in pantomime leads to the next aspect of creative dramatics—improvisation. This part of the art goes back to the very fountainhead of drama, for it was through improvisation that the Dionysian ritual took the first steps which led to the creation of Greek tragedy.[24]

Improvisation often becomes confused with pantomime. The two are closely related, of course, but certain differences are apparent. True improvisation is unplanned and unpredictable and usually calls for a more complicated emerging structure than does mime. Improvisation also includes speech. The only structure provided in full improvisation is the delineation of the opening situation, and sometimes even this is omitted. Sometimes students are given a situation and a description of the characters and their relationships to each other, but no reference is made to personality traits. The actors must then try to be the persons they are playing and to live the situation in which they are involved.

The teacher should be aware of certain characteristics of student improvisation so that as dramatic action emerges he will have a clearer sense of what to expect and where guidance will be helpful. In most instances, early improvisations with students will have an almost complete lack of form. Students will be creating their structure as they proceed, and this structure may not be visible to the casual observer; likewise there may not be a proper beginning, middle, or end as adults often conceive of them. Talk will often run rampant, with students carrying on conversations while the improvisation is in progress. Much of this talk will turn out to be a running commentary on what is to happen next—a method for verbalizing stage directions. Dialogue as it does emerge in improvisation will often falter and sometimes disappear completely; at other times the dialogue may be incomprehensible to all except those who are taking part. And in many cases it may be completely impossible for the casual observer to tell what, if anything, is going on.

None of this should dismay the teacher, for students are in the midst of creating their own structure, their own order, and all this takes time and considerable patience on the part of everyone. Dorothy Heathcote defines improvisation as "discovery by trial, error and testing; using available materials with respect for their nature, and being guided by this appreciation of their potential. The end product of improvisation is the experience of it."[25]

Begun at an early age, extemporizing or improvising can head off later self-consciousness and make verbalization easier and more natural as well as increase an individual's presence of mind and develop his inventiveness.[26] Improvisations provide a special service for experiences in narrative; they translate what happened back to what is happening and promote a sense of immediacy which might otherwise be lacking. This approach becomes quite important for those students who find it difficult to deal with abstractions. With drama they are able to participate in and work with a form of reality that may come much closer to their own experiential backgrounds. For other students the process of improvisation helps to demonstrate the relationship between narrative and drama. Often literature such as myths, fairy tales, and the like is highly condensed and impersonal. A lack of physical detail, dialogue, and personal points of view make the works seem distant and inappropriate. Through improvisation students supply the missing elements and make the stories become a part of their own experience. Stanislavski, the father of modern acting, used improvisation to teach his actors naturalness, inventiveness, and the ability to believe in the make-believe.[27]

As many kinds of improvisations exist as there are materials and situations. The subject matter may be original or it may derive from any number of sources, including any subject field. For instance, a group may wish to dramatize an interview with a person they have studied. The group discusses the life and the qualities of the person, making a list of his accomplishments and characteristics. A variety of situations can be used as settings for interviews. The person might be on television, radio, or at a press conference, and he could be interviewed by a number of individuals representing different factions or purposes.[28]

Another teacher might use improvisation to prepare for reading a book, having the class perform some of the key situations in advance in order to get students involved in the work. Another way would be to create hypothetical situations similar to those which will be read and to ask students to play these through. Following discussion of their improvisations, the class could then read the actual work in question and develop some valuable comparisons and contrasts.[29] Emphasis in both cases would probably be placed more on facts and circumstances than on character traits, at least at the beginning.

Still another approach is to use minimal situations originating with students and opening the way to the eventual writing of plays. A group might improvise an original situation until it meets their satisfaction and then write it down in play format. Or, after group experiences, individuals can be asked to choose minimal situations and write playlets based on them. These minimal situations can be drawn from history, foreign languages—good opportunity for vocabulary development—science, or even certain aspects of mathematics. However, this type of activity usually appears only after students have had ample experience with general improvisation. Rushing them to script writing will produce only mediocre results and could possibly create barriers toward the uses of drama in other situations. Let the desire for script unfold naturally. (Further considerations for handling the scripted situation are discussed later in this chapter.)

Another possible approach is to work with student writing which tends to be highly condensed, expanding the condensed sections through improvisation. Such an activity will help students to see the values and possibilities of greater detailing and specificity in both acting and writing. Interrelationships between writing and improvisation, or any other form of drama, should be stressed whenever possible.

Frequently, though, students are at a loss for materials. For this reason the teacher will often find it desirable to start an improvisation session with a well-chosen story rather than to launch directly into free improvisational work. Students meeting something new often work more effectively if they have a sense of structure to support them. The well-written story offers an excellent skeleton upon which to build; later on, spontaneous, free work undoubtedly will profit from this kind of preliminary experience with form. Age is also a factor here. Younger children, limited in their ability to show characterization by their own immaturity of conception, may need help. More complex materials may be introduced as students grow in maturity.

An important factor in work with derived materials is that students must come to understand the differences between story and drama. In fiction, the appearance, disposition, and behavior of the characters are described; in drama the characters themselves must portray these qualities through pantomime and dialogue. In fiction the place of action is pictured; in drama the setting or the dialogue must suggest the scene. Usually a story informs the reader of what actions are performed, but the play requires that actors perform them; and where a story tells the feelings of an individual, the drama demands that the characters show their emotions when necessary. With these distinctions in mind, the creative dramatics teacher then makes his selection from myths, folklore, fairy tales, historical materials, nature, animal stories, general fiction, autobiography, and life (see suggested sources of materials in the "Handbook of Resources").

Once the teacher discovers a selection which he feels meets the needs and abilities of his students, he proceeds to introduce it to them, usually be reading or telling it. Dewey Chambers suggests that the teacher follow a sequence—outlined below—to achieve best results and maximum participation.

1. Select a good story—and then tell it.
2. With the class, break the plot down into sequences, or scenes, that can be played. Note these on the chalkboard.
3. From those noted on the board, choose a scene, or scenes, to be played.
4. Break the scene, or scenes, into further sequence.
5. Discuss the scene or scenes. Discuss setting, motivation, characterization, the times, physical make-up of characters, etc. Help the children to develop mental images of the characters, what they did, how they did it, why they did it.
6. Choose the players. Let them go into conference and plan in more detail what they will do during the playing period.
7. Plan with the youngsters who remain. Let them know that the play will be re-cast and re-played, and that they might pretend a part in the next playing.
8. Instruct youngsters to watch the play for five things they like and five things that could be improved in the next playing.
9. With an agreed upon signal, start the play. Let it continue until it is finished.
10. Let the players return to their group, and have all evaluate the play, using the criteria in No. 8.
11. Re-cast, instruct remaining students as in No. 8 and re-play the scene.
12. Evaluate. If time permits, re-cast and re-play.[30]

Chambers' approach is highly structured, and not every teacher will find it necessary to approach improvisational work in this way. But the essentials of Chambers' approach are important: selection of material, selection of scenes, assigning of roles, the preparation of the audience— if there is one—and evaluation. The entire process appears as if it would take a great deal of time, but the actual preparation period is quite short, and the playing time likewise tends to be short. This is an advantage, for then more students can participate and there will be several versions to evaluate. Gradually students will accept the work of going through the preparatory stages on their own until they are able to devise and carry through their dramatic work from inception to completion with little aid from the teacher.

Problems will arise as students are accepting this process. One of these falls in the area of characterization. Both younger and older students will tend at first to play stereotypes. With younger students, a gradual process of developing convincing characterizations through questions, evaluation, and frequent dramatic experience will prove best in most instances. With the secondary school student, depending upon his maturity and his ability, it may be necessary to follow the same procedure; or he may be able to see, with some guidance, what the various stages of growth in characterization are as they apply to him. Some authorities such as Brian Way have claimed that definite stages of understanding character are a part of students' growing maturity. Way outlines these stages in the following fashion:

1. The intuitive and unconscious exploration of characters of the inner world of fantasy and imagination.
2. The largely unconscious exploration of characters (both of fantasy and of the real world) in action.
3. The beginnings of exploration of the cause and effects of the actions of characters; there is still a particular interest in action, but a growing awareness of the causes and effects of that action in its external relationship to broad characteristics of people. Here, intellectual considerations begin to impinge on the physical-emotional realms; characterization begins to be, as does drama as a whole, more conscious.
4. The exploration not only of the external factors of causes and effects but also of the inner factors (motivations) of the actions of characters; this is part of a fully conscious form of intended creation of characters with, quite often, no major interest in action as such; it is a realm of drama that, again in general terms, belongs only to secondary education, and possibly only from about fourteen years onwards. By this stage, with proper growth arising from natural and organic opportunity, there is a balanced use of the physical, emotional and intellectual self.[31]

Once aware of these stages of growth, the teacher can help students reach for further development. Alert for signs that students are exploring their relation to characterization, the instructor will suggest activities that will promote greater appreciation of character.

A second major problem that arises frequently during creative work involves dialogue. At first students will tend to stumble as they develop dialogue, and there will be many times when dialogue simply evaporates. This happens because students are struggling to match action with dialogue, and the balancing act required often calls for more than they can give at that time. James Moffett feels that speech is vital to any dramatic development, but he also knows that "when anyone verbalizes solo fashion, whether silently to himself, aloud to another, or on paper to the world, he must draw on discourse he has heard, had and read. A student can give to the world only some permutation of what he got from the world."[32] Hence we should not be disturbed when students often "run out of speech" while dramatizing. Moffett suggests that in the classroom students can be helped with vocal development if different kinds of dialogue are created in which questioning, collaborating, and qualifying are normal operations.[33] Many students slowly will come to the point where their conversations in drama approach the spontaneous, ongoing, and unpondered style of real-life conversation.

It is important to provide situations in which the students' capacity for imaginative concentration is developed to the point where they recognize the need to speak. First attempts will often be quite mediocre, but if the dramatic situations are real to the students, improvement will soon be evident.[34] As students gain confidence in their speaking abilities, such skills as tonal variation and speech pace can become a part of their work. Simple exercises combining movement and speech often work well. For instance, students might be asked to render certain phrases and sentences in such a way as to suggest various qualities of action. Some examples would include "They strolled slowly down the street"; "He leaped from the path of the car"; "Stretching first one arm, then the other, then his legs, he finally raised himself out of bed." From simple exercises like this, groups of four could then work on lines such as "They squealed on us," or "I told you we should have done it another way."[35] No one, of course, can lay down rigid rules for developing tonal design, but usually tonal forms follow the shape of the physical movements with which they are associated. Students' speech skills take on added dimension when such relationships are made clear.

Combining these activities into an overall program should provide ample opportunity for students to develop both speech and dramatic skills. As students come to explore the possibilities of a text or a situation, discussions of interpretations arise, fostering further speech experience in the classroom as well as developing attitudes of discrimination and inference. Frequently, by improvising the instances that come up in small group discussions, the students can go from generalities to examples; and by discussing the material of the improvisations in small groups again, they can go from examples back to generalities. In this way students become used to moving among levels of abstraction, an important part of their educational development.

Gradually increasing the use of minimal situations, some of which involve moral, psychological, or social issues, the teacher will help students move into topic-centered discussions as well. At first, as students concentrate on action, conversation about themes may be incidental, but eventually the teacher may propose a situation in which characters are basically just sitting around and talking about some issue on which they have to make a decision. The scene is still dramatic because students continue in fictive roles and the talk is story-action. This type of improvisation, which can become quite sophisticated, leads to spontaneous discussions where fictive roles along with the story action are dropped and the true discussion begins.[36]

Discussion, then, is a type of oral improvisation in itself. Students accept and play certain roles; they evaluate how others in the group are reacting to them and how they themselves are reacting to others. The motives behind people's speech become important, and students scan closely the corresponding body English and tonal design to receive as many clues as possible to perform valid evaluations of others' intentions and to determine responses. Any class is a miniature communication system which develops its own communicative signals, its own atmosphere, and its own control of space and movement. If the members pay attention to its workings and are introduced to the various aspects which constitute its operation, they can learn more about what makes and breaks communication than any textbook on the subject can get across.

Above all else, the teacher must let students find their own levels of achievement as they proceed from simple to more complex dramatic work. If, however, the teacher receives examples such as the following during improvisational work, he may congratulate himself and know that students are making good progress toward being able to cope with unusual situations and emerging characterization. In this particular instance the following situation was given to the students: you are a young lady with a toothache and you go out to find a dentist; but owing to the blackout (it is wartime) you get into the office of an undertaker. The children involved in this sketch were British students about thirteen years old. Here is the record of their improvisation.

> She enters looking very miserable. He says, "Well madam, what can I do for you?"
> "This is terrible."
> "I know, madam, these sufferings are difficult to bear. Tell me about it."
> "I think it's decaying."
> "Good Lord, how long have you had it?"
> "About a month."
> "But this is absurd. Haven't you done anything about it?"
> "I tried stuffing it with cottonwool."
> "But, madam, you must have it removed."
> "I refuse to have it removed unless you promise to give me a gold plate."
> "Sorry, madam, but we only make brass plates."
> "But it will go all verdigris!"
> "That, madam, will not matter. No one will see it."[37]

Role Playing

A special aspect of improvisation which has received considerable publicity is role playing; it probably constitutes the one section of creative dramatics with which a large number of teachers are at least acquainted. However, as Jean Grambs says, "Despite the years in which we have talked about role-playing, demonstrated it, won devotees (for the moment), you cannot name any teachers you know who routinely use role-playing as a way of teaching."[38]

There are a number of reasons for this failure to apply role playing in the classroom. First is the confusion about what role playing actually is. In real life people have expectations about their own behavior and that of others; hence a man may act like a student in an evening university course, like a father with his own children, like a boss at his place of work, and even like a teacher, should the need arise. All of us play roles in life, and according to Peter L. Berger, sociologist, we define these roles in the following way:

> A role, then, may be defined as a typified response to a typified expectation. Society has predefined the fundamental typology. To use the language of the theater, from which the concept of role is derived, we can say that society provides the script for all the *dramatis personae*. The individual actors... need but slip into the roles already assigned to them before the curtain goes up. As long as they play their roles as provided for in this script, the social play can proceed as planned.[39]

Role playing, then, as it is used in creative drama, is, in its simplest form, the practice or experience of "being someone else." In another sense, however, role playing is a generic term which provides an umbrella-like cover for a number of variations. Raymond Corsini has selected four connotations that may be applied to role playing.

1. *Theatrical*—plays following a script simulate reality for the purpose of entertainment
2. *Sociological*—patterns of behavior as dictated by social norms
3. *Dissimulative*—deceptive behavior in which one tries to fool others by acting in a manner contrary to real intentions, emotions, or motivations
4. *Educational*—people act out imaginary situations for purposes directed to self-understanding, improvement of skills, analysis of behavior; or to demonstrate to others how one operates or how one should operate.[40]

We are, of course, primarily concerned with the educational version of role playing; but the question arises as to what value role playing has in creative dramatics. Role playing brings to students a procedure that allows them to explore their feelings about the situations in life which most fundamentally shape their attitudes and values. But other advantages appear as well. Role playing provides an extremely close representation of real-life behavior without the attendant dangers of such behavior; the individual becomes involved holistically and presents observers—though not in the true sense an audience—a picture of how the individual operates in a real-life situation. Because role playing is dramatic, it focuses attention on problems relating to personality as well as society. And, most importantly, participation in role playing permits the individual to see himself while in action in a neutral situation. He can come to a better comprehension of his abilities to cope with varied situations and also develop a clearer awareness of what his weaknesses may be.[41]

The teacher who decides to use role playing with his classes should be quite familiar with the process before undertaking its direct application to the classroom environment. Although the group defines, examines, and tries to solve its own problems, the teacher is present to help the students learn to do the job through the use of this tool. Therefore, before trying role playing with his students, it is advisable that the teacher explore the practice with colleagues or friends who are interested in the role-playing process. Ideally, teachers should secure the advice of someone who has used role playing successfully.

Once the teacher has some confidence in the technique and in his own ability to use it, he is ready to introduce it into the classroom. The teacher may find it helpful to work with small groups first, keeping the situations very simple and structuring the approaches somewhat until he gains confidence in the process and sees that students comprehend the necessary procedures. In most cases, role playing works best in a problem-solving situation. Students, of course, find that any type of problem solving tends to be a difficult task. Learning to weigh the effects of a course of action, making choices in terms of democratic values, and then acting in accordance with those values usually take time and require considerable judgment and social sensitivity. Teachers are well advised to avoid tense or emotionally threatening situations with a class that has had no experience in reflecting on its own behavior through role playing.

In general, though, certain steps to the role playing process may be followed to insure a sense of continuity and worthwhile development. Naturally the first step is the selection of a problem. The topic should be clear, specific, and not too complex. The subject should be one that can be handled by the particular group in question, and it should offer potential for solutions that group members are capable of reaching without fear of feeling inadequate. To insure a measure of personal security and privacy, students might begin by focusing on issues of a general nature involving role behavior itself.

Locating the actual material or problem can be done in a number of ways. One is to let students use a problem consensus—students list some of the common problem situations they have experienced or which are characteristic of the material being studied; from these, several are selected and then explored for their potential. Students should be encouraged to select material from subject areas, since working within the framework of a subject often helps to minimize attention to personal problems and keeps the roles separated in students' minds. History, for example, is an excellent source of materials, although historical role playing often calls for prior planning and research.[42] For instance, the problems might be centered around some of the following general situations:

1. A committee of the Constitutional Convention attempts to determine the effects of the Negro population upon congressional representation.
2. A congressional committee debates the "free speech" amendment or any other amendment of the Bill of Rights.
3. President Jefferson and selected advisers discuss the wisdom and constitutionality of the Louisiana purchase.

Other sources might be drawn from science; these could focus on social issues and are likely to overlap into sociodrama (to be discussed later). Here is how the teacher might set up role playing in certain aspects of science.

Area of study: Biology, General Science, Hygiene

Possible situation: The mayor of a small town has become concerned about the high incidence of rats in his community. To stamp out the problem requires money—more than the town has available. The mayor attempts to elicit the help of his U.S. senator, a man who has been notoriously unconcerned about the problems of the average city dweller.

Concepts to be learned or stressed: The threat of rats as carriers of disease; importance of sanitation; importance to community, state, and country of maintaining standards for good health.

Area of study: Biology, Hygiene

Possible situation: During the course of a meal in a restaurant, a diner notices that his waiter's hands are dirty, that the silverware has not been properly washed, and that the washroom has a dirty roller-type towel.

Concepts to be learned or stressed: Lack of cleanliness in food preparation can cause disease; importance of inspection standards and licensing arrangements; the operation of bureaus such as the FDA.

Area of study: Biology

Possible situation: Four members of a class are chosen to represent (1) a doctor, (2) a science teacher, (3) a law enforcement official, and (4) a user of drugs. The individuals engage in a discussion of whether or not the user of drugs should be punished, what effects drug consumption may have on the human body, what effects drug users have on society in general, etc. The situation could be made more dramatic by having the scene set in a courtroom and changing the roles slightly.[43]

There should be little difficulty developing problem situations in foreign languages, industrial education, business, and other subject areas. In most instances it is far better to have the students supply the problems which they feel are most pressing and most directly related to their backgrounds. George and Fannie Shaftel suggest that problems should relate to intergroup needs, and they cite the following as some of the most predominant of those needs.

1. Concern about inequalities
2. Understanding that people are what they are because of their experiences
3. Awareness of patterns of behavior
4. Acceptance of duties as citizens
5. Attitudes of respect for culture, religions, and institutions of others
6. Knowledge that members of a group are interdependent.[44]

Still another source for material is the problem story. A detailed plot is to be avoided, for it would tend to become a cage which would inhibit the emotional identification of the players with the roles they are assuming. Not just any story will do for role playing. The Shaftels recommended the following characteristics:

1. The story is intended to be read aloud to a group and should be written for easy reading.
2. The reading time should be from ten to twenty minutes; even longer stories, however, can be effective.
3. Each story is based upon a developmental task of the age of the group for which it is planned. The story is not finished; it comes to a stop at the highest possible peak of intensity in the form of a dilemma which presents various alternatives for action. This is a crucial element of the story. Impetus for discussion must lie in the various choices of possible behavior for solving the problems of human relations basic to the story.
4. The story must be effective as drama. That is, it must create an illusion which catches and holds the audience's interest intensely. Every possible dramatic device of humor, irony and surprise should be used to make the story a worthwhile aesthetic experience.
5. The story must have complete conviction for the audience for which it is intended. Tone, vocabulary, and the issues involved must be realistic; to achieve the deeply felt "identification" of audience with story characters that is so necessary as impetus for whole-hearted role-playing.[45]

Once the problem or material has been selected, the teacher still has some responsibility in determining which alternatives presented by the students offer dramatic possibilities and then guiding the students in the direction of the approaches which seem most fruitful. If many alternatives are supplied by students, a selection may be made and other choices held in abeyance for further playing. Eventually the teacher should be able to discard even this "selecting" role as students become more adept at spotting the potential drama within situations.

The warm-up follows the selection of the problem. Plunging into a role-playing scene without preliminary warm-up can cause the actual role playing to fail, for students need time to acclimate themselves to the problem and to the various roles. Hence in the warm-up the actual "facts" of the scene to be played begin to appear; site, general characteristics, and broad courses of action develop through questions and discussion. In general, students become better acquainted with the demands of the problem, and they begin to focus emotionally and intellectually on the specific situation, which in turn helps them to begin identifying with the individual roles and the conflict inherent in the problem. Sometimes the warm-up is very brief and simply consists of the teacher and students asking questions of the various characters to help them get into their roles. Some teachers like to have a quick run-through of a similar situation in order to prepare students for the situation at hand. Such a practice is debatable, however, on the grounds that it tends to take too much time and may distract rather than involve the students in the selected problem. Careful questioning and delineation of the scene are usually sufficient for effective participation.

Once the warm-up is well under way, the selection of the players is the next step; actually the two—warm-up and selection—may occur simultaneously. Keeping the number of players small at the beginning is a good idea, for having too many actors at once tends to obscure and confuse the issue. The selection process can be crucial to the success of the role playing; for that reason it may be a good idea to start with the more stable and socially accepted students and gradually work toward involvement of others. However, placing a child in his usual life role should be avoided because the identification problems which can result are not always beneficial. In the selection of players, David Potter and Martin Andersen suggest five general criteria: (1) do not force a person to play a role; (2) do not make the selection at random; (3) try to select people who will participate seriously in the role play; (4) do not select people for a role in which they are deeply involved emotionally; (5) do not carry out the selection as if trying out for parts in a regular play. [46]

Some people favor volunteer casting, but certain drawbacks exist with this, at least initially. Frequently the most articulate will volunteer, and they may need the experience least. Many students will not choose roles that will help them most, and it is difficult to get people to volunteer for unpopular or difficult roles. The class may be asked, however, to give suggestions, and from these, certain additional selections can be made. When students have had considerable experience in role playing and have learned what is needed, they will usually be able to handle the selection process by themselves with quite satisfactory results. Those students who still remain reluctant to act often may serve as consultants to the actors, advising them on possible interpretations of the roles.

Once the selection of roles has been accomplished, the next procedure is to prepare the rest of the group to function as an audience. Although it is not always desirable in creative drama to separate performer and observer, it is not always detrimental to have this division in the role-playing situation. Often circumstances such as time, space, and situation dictate it. Therefore, the teacher must be aware of the important part the audience plays in making a role-playing experience a successful one. A number of ways to involve the audience in the role playing are available. Certain segments of the audience may be given specific tasks to do. In general these tasks fall under the headings of listening, watching, explaining, and consulting. For instance, under such categories the students might be asked to consider some of the following:

1. Note what actually takes place in comparison to the outlined situation.
2. Try to determine the feelings of the role players as they enact their roles.
3. Note actions that aid in resolving the problem situation or in blocking its resolution.
4. Note how a specific role player develops his part.
5. Determine the motivations for the actions of the role players.
6. Try to imagine how the role players might have acted to resolve the problem more quickly.
7. Note whether the problem situation as enacted had any similarities to human-relations problems in other areas of life.[47]

The basic principle behind audience preparation is that students who are not acting must feel they have a specific function to fulfill, or the discussion following the enactment will tend to be vague and unhelpful for everyone concerned.

The actual playing of the scene should be rapid, but this does not always happen. Sometimes the action will start quickly, while at other times it must be prompted by questions—"How does your character feel? What would he do now? How would he reply to that statement?" Gauging time is one of the teacher's most difficult tasks, but adequate time should be allowed for the students to become involved in the action. The teacher must not let the scene drag on until students lose interest; neither should he cut it so short that the problem is not presented effectively.

As the action unfolds, some falling out of role should be expected. No actor is expected to be flawless, and too much censorship in this regard dampens spontaneity. Students should be helped to see that the way an actor portrays a role is no reflection upon him as a person. He is simply acting out a characterization as he sees it. While the playing is going on, the teacher may want to raise certain questions. It is permissible to interrupt briefly to redirect, but it is equally important not to embarrass the players. Attention also has to be given to whether or not students are under too much pressure and whether or not they feel threatened. Sudden retreat from a position, expressions of sudden anger, unusual flushing, and crying are possible indications that the pressure has become too great. If such signs do appear, the playing should be interrupted and either redirected or moved on to discussion and evaluation.

Once students become well acquainted with the procedures of role playing, certain additional techniques can be introduced during the playing which sometimes help to heighten awareness of the dramatic situation. For instance, some students may act as alter egos for the players.[48] The primary purpose of role playing is to see one's own behavior in a new perspective, and the use of the alter ego enhances this process. Basically, the alter ego identifies with the character but does not feel personally responsible for him. The relationship may be started by having the alter ego tell the actor what to do and how to react. Then the role could be changed so that the alter ego explains what his character's real feelings and attitudes are—these may or may not correspond with the actions of the actor. The resulting added dimension to character portrayal illuminates different factors of personality and character development which might otherwise be overlooked. However, the alter-ego practice takes great concentration and confidence; consequently it should be introduced only when the students feel quite secure in their roles and have had extensive experience in the role-playing process.

Another valuable device is the soliloquy. Students meet this in formal drama, though they may not be fully aware of it. The actor interrupts the action and talks directly to the class—reflecting out loud on how the character being played feels or thinks. In this way the actor supplies the audience with more information and at the same time reveals more of his character to the other players. An alternative to this, similar to the alter ego, is the double identity who is involved right along with the actor and enters the conversation when the play is stopped briefly. This person expresses his impressions of the character's private thoughts and reactions, rather than his observable actions and statements. Such a role does not come easily, and the majority of students will never reach the stage where they are able to take on the double-identity role.[49]

Still another helpful device is the role reversal. A sudden switch to play an opposite role maximizes the effect of placing one's self in someone else's shoes. To operate within the framework of the other person and to have to solve as another character the very problems he himself has created forces the student to sharpen and extend his comprehension of the problem situation.

A fourth device is the auxiliary chair. Frequently used in therapy work, it may prove useful on occasion in the classroom. Chairs are used to represent various types of characters or behaviors that are part of the problem to be solved. Feelings, actions, and thoughts or terms that might be assigned to a person are assigned instead to the chairs. Responses characteristic of these behaviors can be verbally expressed by the teacher while he stands behind the chair—students then behave toward the chair as if it were really exhibiting the behaviors. Such an approach should be employed with extreme caution, however, for students may confuse the teacher and the chair, and the resulting complications in behavior can create definite problems.[50]

Once the playing has been completed, the most important aspect of role playing remains—discussion and evaluation. This aspect is vital to the gradual separation of role and reality in the minds of students; without it, considerable uncertainty may result, and students could carry roles further than they realize. The process of getting information about the effects of one's role behavior is called feedback. This feedback can come in a variety of ways but it *should come*. During the discussion following the role playing, students must discover the separation between dramatic role and reality. Simple comments by the teacher such as "How does the role compare to other roles in life? What other ways might the role have been played?" help set the tone of the discussion as well as its focus. Use role names whenever possible rather than real ones; this minimizes any direct threat that a student might feel from criticism which occurs during the discussion sessions.

In addition to the various questions and tasks that were assigned to the audience before the role playing began, some basic considerations for the class to examine during the discussion include the following: (1) How did the characters feel as they were acting their roles? (2) What was needed in the situation which was not supplied? (3) Why did the different players respond in the ways they did? Emphasis placed on the positive ways of solving the problem and frequent encouragement and appreciation given to the actors will keep the discussion atmosphere open. The main thrust of the discussion should center on the essential issues involved and the relationship of those issues to the students' experiences.

The teacher himself may wish to perform an evaluation of the effectiveness of role playing with his students. He can choose a number of ways to do this. One would be to take notes during the playing, focusing on such items as which students are most actively interested in the playing, who appears to be listening and reacting, which students are fairly inattentive, and which ones are actively resisting participation and tend to disrupt the proceedings. A series of notations about his students over a period of time can offer a teacher considerable insight as to the progress a class is making in dramatic activity and understanding.

The teacher might elect to use evaluation forms, but only after students are quite skilled at playing. Chesler and Fox recommend the following general categories for use in evaluating performances.

1. *Very poor*—has great difficulty remaining in role; lacks feeling for role; shows little interest in developing role
2. *Poor*—has some difficulty staying in role; playing tends toward the superficial; shows little spontaneity
3. *Average*—remains in role most of the time; demonstrates some feeling for role; lacks creativity in developing different aspects of role
4. *Good*—stays in role quite consistently; demonstrates ability to change roles; shows some creativity in developing roles
5. *Very good*—appears at ease in various roles; develops role beyond outline given in briefing; exhibits behavior and feelings appropriate for role.[51]

Such a rating scale should be used only to keep a record of how students are progressing, not as a record for grading purposes. No one should receive the impression that he is being graded on his acting ability during his participation in role playing, or any other form of creative dramatic activity.

The best evaluation develops from class discussion. Here students reveal a great deal about their degree of involvement and growth in dramatic skill as well as about their social understanding. Also out of these discussions will come suggestions for improvement in procedures, new situations to be explored, and a better view of students' interests and experiences.

We have indicated that role playing is a generic term which covers a variety of activities; one variation, called sociodrama, has proven popular with educators in several subject fields. The basic distinction between sociodrama and the role playing we have been discussing is that the former is concerned with the effect that usual, acceptable, normal behavior has upon people when they interact with each other in normal situations. Sociodrama, then, places primary emphasis on social problems and draws more on types and patterns of behavior than on individuals. Hence sociodrama allows the teacher to explore with students their attitudes about such areas as home, neighborhood, and peer relations, which usually do not enter classroom experience.[52]

The basic methods for using sociodrama are the same as those for regular role playing. Situations sometimes differ, however. For example, a group studying international problems might adopt the roles of some of the principals in an international dispute in order to gain insights into the forces involved. Such exercises as the model U.N. assemblies held in some parts of the country for high school students are a form of sociodramatic activity. Another situation might grow from a court decision. For example, black students or white students will be entering a new school which previously has not been integrated. To reduce barriers that might appear between the old and the new students, a situation can be created which dramatizes some of the problems. Starting outside the racial framework and working with just the idea of new students in class should be sufficient to raise some of the issues and questions which could be encountered in the real-life situation. Still another possibility for sociodramatic activity can be found in class programs of study. For example, a voter registration campaign is being conducted soon in a community. Students from social studies classes have decided to conduct a community-wide survey of people's political interests and attitudes, and this will entail interviews with a number of people. Role playing an appropriate interview would be excellent preparation for the project.

Behavior and social problems, however, are the basis of most sociodrama, and the teacher can use this approach to learn what problems need clarification, what relationships are difficult, and what stereotypes need changing.[53] Most improvisation/role playing with adolescents and even younger children reveals considerable confusion about adult-child relationships. Some basic situations which might help bring these problems into the open include the following:

1. A teacher unfairly accuses a student of cheating during an examination.

2. A teenager comes home two hours after he has told his parents he will be home. They are waiting for him.

3. A high school student is applying for a summer job during a time when jobs are scarce and he has little experience to offer.

4. A clerk has overcharged a person and the latter is discussing the matter with him.

5. A student believes his examination grade is incorrect due to an error on the part of the teacher; he is talking to his instructor about it.

6. A very conscientious student who is afraid to do anything irregular has loaned his term paper notes to a classmate. After the term papers are passed in, the teacher calls the first student

into his office and accuses him of plagiarism. How does the student resolve the problem? How does the teacher resolve it?

Teachers in various subject fields will find that sociodrama offers at least one way to deal with problems that may be of utmost concern to students but which would otherwise slip by and continue to create problems in the classroom.[54]

For the non-academic student in particular, role playing of any type provides opportunities for demonstrating capabilities and skills which would otherwise go unnoticed. Students discover that their feelings are not "crazy" or "weird" but are shared by many others in the group, even the teacher. Here again one of the basic purposes of drama appears: the provision of a secure atmosphere in which to experiment with new roles and feelings in a person's own life.

A great temptation to moralize exists in role playing; this should be avoided as much as possible when employing improvisational techniques. The chief contribution of role playing in changing behavior is that the solution to the problem lies in the understanding of the situation itself rather than in an abstraction about what is right or wrong.[55] The only generalization that will actually modify behavior is that which comes from insight. This takes time, and often we must be thankful if we merely start the process of feeling and thinking. One cannot role play a situation on only one occasion and expect results. It must be repeated on many occasions in varied forms, and children should be given the opportunity to play any or all parts in the drama until the whole situation becomes familiar to them.

The inexperienced teacher needs to be warned, however, that role playing has its dangers. Above all, the regular teacher should not make the mistake of considering himself on an equal basis with the trained psychiatrist, physician, or counselor, nor should he direct his role playing exercises for such purposes. But the classroom teacher does not need to be a psychologist to use role playing at the instructional and interpersonal levels. As long as the problems used are treated as sociodrama or the focus is placed on typical roles, problems, and situations that students usually face, little difficulty should arise. Nevertheless, the teacher will have to be alert to avoid involving himself and his classes in portrayals and interpretations that seriously impinge upon psychological privacy and security.

Of course, in any group enterprise of this type, even in ordinary discussion, it may happen that a person will expose himself to ridicule or rejection by being too frank about himself and his feelings before others are ready to accept them. Often in the heat of a debate, when a permissive atmosphere has been established, a young person will reveal some past behavior which will hurt his status among his peers. But a safeguard against damage to an individual's self-image is built into role playing, for it is self-limiting in at least one sense. If discussion or acting cuts into painful areas, the group will tend to shrink away defensively, closing in self-protection, and the session will soon come to a halt. The teacher who is alert and empathizes with his students will recognize the signs and take steps to move the session in less threatening directions.

A number of criticisms have been leveled against role playing. In the first place people tend to think it is too artificial, that the only way students are going to learn about life is to go out and live it and take their chances. No one will deny that the school of hard knocks is an effective teacher, but it can also be a damaging one. Role playing in a classroom environment provides a means for students to test and explore without threat of failure and without permanent personal damage and loss of self-esteem, which so often occur in real life. Role playing is not actual life-living; it is only an approximation. But it is an approximation which may help students prepare to cope with the real actions of life when they do occur. It is also said that role playing is superficial and that students do not achieve any depth of perception. Initially this can be true, but as students proceed to use the various techniques of role playing more skillfully, their perceptions deepen and their ability to cope with expanded problems increases.

The following excerpt from a student role-playing session offers evidence of this increasing perception. The problem that students were wrestling with was that of a boy who wished to attend rehearsals for a play but who was having difficulty persuading his father that the activity was all right and that he would not be running around the streets with a wild bunch of people. Students worked on the problem in groups and came up with many solutions, but the following one, in which the boy begins to ask the father questions about the father's idea of responsibility, seems to offer the best example of this deepening perception.

> "All right, then, what do I have to do to be responsible?"
> "What do you mean, what do you have to do? I already told you. And you can't go to the play."
> "No, I mean what, exactly what do I have to do? Tell me some things that I could do to show you that I was responsible."
> (The father was clearly taken aback). "Well," he sputtered, "you, you, you have to clean up your room."
> "OK, I can do that."
> "And you haven't been doing a good job of the dishes. You never wipe off the sink."
> "Yeah, I'm sorry. I forget. But if you feel that way about it, I'll make sure I remember."
> "And, and—why don't you get your hair cut?"[56]

Students recognized the prejudice and were able to discuss intelligently how stereotypes get in the way of communication. In this way, role playing can lead to the development of intellectual perception.

Critics also charge that students lack the experience to play roles intelligently. But one never begins with the unknown in role playing; he proceeds from the known to the unknown, building from a present base of knowledge and learning as he goes, drawing upon others in his group, doing research as he discovers his weak areas. When a student sees his lack of knowledge in an area, he is often spurred to find answers, to supply information which he may not have been aware of. But for this to happen, the original situation must be rooted in his own experience. Hence as a stimulus for additional learning, role playing—and dramatic activity as a whole—seems to offer an excellent approach.

In general, then, if the teacher keeps in mind the following principles as he works with students and role playing, he should avoid most of the criticisms and find himself working with an exciting and meaningful teaching experience.

1. Role playing requires time; discussion and reenactment are as important as initial playing.
2. Role playing is a method, not an end.
3. The group should be concerned with the problem being enacted, not the individuals performing.
4. Keep clear of therapy for therapy's sake.
5. Keep the role playing democratic; involve students in all steps.
6. Resist telling answers to students; role playing is part of the process of discovery.
7. Do not set up role playing situations so that there is only one possible answer; the purpose of role playing is to explore alternatives.
8. If you do not know the group well, be alert lest you as a leader are used to put someone on the spot.
9. Avoid problems that do not belong to the group or that do not fit within their experiential background.
10. Role playing is not merely a means of entertaining; present it as a means for analysis and study of real human relations problems.
11. Avoid forcing the technique on a group; prepare the members for role playing before using it; breakdown of resistance comes slowly; approach new ways of problem solving gradually.
12. Remember that the problem analysis is the main step in a role playing sequence. Do not be seduced by the desires of role players to perfect a scene; finished acting is neither necessary nor desirable.[57]

It may appear that role playing is really the only form of improvisation. Such is not the case, for other aspects of improvisation may be found in the use of puppetry, shadow plays, and radio plays.

These approaches are usually used with younger children to overcome their sensitivity about acting, but they may be employed effectively at any level.

Puppets, for example, act as masks which enable players to feel freer in their actions. They are particularly helpful when children are extremely self-conscious or because of some kind of handicap do not move easily. Puppetry is also an excellent approach to use when space limitations make it difficult for an entire group to participate at once. Older students often enjoy developing puppet plays for younger children; this can be an intermediate step for some who hesitate about joining their own group's dramatic activity immediately. If the teacher knows something about the art of puppetry, he can develop many activities; but this knowledge is not essential since children usually respond well to this kind of dramatization and are perfectly willing to employ a suspension of disbelief for the purpose. Even simple paper bag puppets created in a short time make an adequate mask with which many children will perform satisfactorily.[58]

Shadow plays are dramatizations performed behind a translucent screen—usually a sheet stretched tautly across a frame—with the shadows of the players thrown into relief by strong back-lighting. Students perform just as if they had no screen in front of them; the security of the shield, however, often helps those who are somewhat inhibited in their action. The possibilities for spontaneous and creative dialogue in puppetry and shadow plays are the same as in regular informal dramatics. The major drawback with shadow plays is the fewer opportunities for experimentation with the way feelings affect bodily movement.[59]

The radio play, actually another manifestation of the puppet play, has some characteristics of shadow drama as well, but the principal emphasis is upon dialogue. Groups with cramped quarters or with a room offering little privacy may find the radio play a good medium. When considering dialogue, students may find the radio play a helpful format. The process of constructing a radio play is much the same as that for dramatizing a regular story except that actions must be conveyed through sound and dialogue; essentials include the presence of suspense, active characterization and, of course, lively dialogue. Plots may be drawn from life, literature, soap operas, movies, and the like. The high school language laboratory is a natural for the production room, and classes can be easily tuned into a program. Students who are electronically inclined should find this a medium that stimulates their inventiveness.[60]

Improvisation, then, offers the teacher many avenues of approach. Its values are numerous, particularly in its emphasis upon exploring differences between two-way and three-way relationships, pace and rhythm, language styles of speakers, settings and circumstances, as well as the dynamics of student interaction.[61] The only limitations are those incurred by lack of imagination, space, time, and certain forms of resistance which students must overcome to reach the state of spontaneity. J. L. Moreno cites four forms of resistance which the actor must be prepared to meet. These are (1) resistance which comes from the actor's bodily actions in the presentation of a role; (2) resistance which comes from his private personality in the production of ideas; (3) resistance that stems from bodily actions, ideas, and emotions of other actors working with him; and (4) resistance that comes from the audience.[62]

Our concern with drama has shown that children are eager to play any story that is in the least way dramatic, but often long before the dramatization has been completed, the class has moved on to a new phase of study. It is unwise, therefore, to attempt too many long and involved dramatizations. Instead one should employ an occasional, rather ambitious dramatic experience as a culmination for large units of work, retaining short dramatic exercises for frequent classroom experiences.[63]

It does not follow that once a student reaches the stage of improvisation he has no need to work with the earlier aspects of creative dramatics. A continuous program should be maintained, with students engaging in all sorts of dramatic activity even as they are progressing to more complex tasks. Brian Way recommends a regular program of activity which will help students keep skills fresh and remind them of the interrelationships which exist between such aspects of drama as sound, movement, pantomime, and improvisation. The guidelines below are offered as a means for developing such an integral program.

1. Regular practice of concentration through the use of the senses (good as warm-up for any activity).
2. Regular practice at using the senses to stimulate the imagination.
3. Regular use of the imagination to stimulate both the use of the body and the use of language (movement and speech).
4. Regular use of movement to stimulate further awareness of and mastery of the physical self and that physical self within its environment.
5. Regular use of speech in order to communicate one's own ideas and feelings to other people (not an audience) and to be able to listen to the ideas and feelings communicated by others (not an audience).
6. Regular practice at becoming aware of other people in order to stimulate and develop sensitivity.
7. Regular practice at using that sensitivity to control one's own emotions (self-discipline and social awareness).

8. Regular practice at using one's emotional self (in harmonious relation to the other facets of oneself) in order to discover more about oneself and other people (developing horizons and broadening experience).[64]

Scripted Plays

One final development remains to be mentioned. Frequent use of improvisation often leads to the development of fully scripted plays. More noticeable perhaps in the field of English, scripted plays may appear in other fields as well. The development toward playwriting ordinarily follows a fairly standard sequence in a child's growth. First comes the regular play of the child followed by dramatic play; this, in turn, leads to improvisations followed by polished improvisations with some words written down; then come stories and dialogues copied from films, television, radio, and life experiences. As expression improves and the ability to write keeps pace, the desire to combine the two—acting and writing—becomes apparent. From this evolves the natural motivation for the written script.[65] However, emphasis upon performance for public reaction in the usual sense should be avoided at the lower levels. The age of thirteen and beyond is usually an appropriate time to introduce the idea of public performance, although some British educators would not have this happen until a child is nearly eighteen.[66]

Ordinarily students will begin with short plays of one scene and then go on to plays which involve multiple scenes and four or five characters. The following sample scripts represent possible outcomes of an early assignment in writing a short script, that of making up a minimal situation playable in about five minutes. The first two were written by disadvantaged students in the seventh and eight grades; the last was done by a boy about to enter seventh grade.

1. Put him in the pot and cook him.
2. O.K. You can have it.
1. That nasty creature.
2. What do you mean, nasty? I got my toe missing because of that.
1. I don't care if it bit your head. Get it out of here.
2. O.K. But the next time I'll be back with a shark.
1. You do and I'll get a whale.

1. Did you spill some tonic on me?
2. Sorry, accidents will happen, sister.
1. That was no accident. You did it on purpose.
2. It happens to the best of us and you're not the best. So shut up and do the dishes.

Situation: You want to go to the ballgame but you don't want to take your little brother.

Scene: Saturday afternoon warm and beautiful day for baseball.

Jack: Mom, I'm going to the ballgame.
Mom: Alright (*overheard by little brother*)
Joe: Can I go with you Jack, please
Jack: No!!!
Mom: *Who* the hell is doing that Hollering
Joe: Jack is. He won't take me to the ballgame.
Jack: Man, he's always going with me. I didn't go with him when he went to Brocton.
Mom: I know but you know how he likes the Yankees.
Jack: I don't give a da— darn who he likes.
Mom: I dare you to swear and I'll whip your ass so bad you won't go to the ballgame at all.
Jack: Alright I'll take him give me his money
Mom: Go get my pocketbook (*Joe goes to get it*)
Joe: Mom I can't find it
Mom: Oh shit I left it in the back seat of the car and your father took the car.
Jack: Dats tooo bad (*he says to Joe like a baby and giggles*)
Joe: (*crying*) Ma you're stupid
Mom: (*with belt in hand whips Joe*) How dare you you bastard.
Jack: So long Mom I be back after the game.[67]

Since short published plays for junior high school youngsters are not numerous, students can be encouraged to write their own. It is a good idea if each writer is a member of the group that will produce his play. A significant feature of this arrangement is that actors and directors can consult with the author concerning various script problems from which the entire group can learn. Students may be unable to read the author's handwriting or to tell how to read a line from the way he has punctuated it. Perhaps they are unsure about the timing of the actions or what kind of a person a character should be, or even what the point of a certain speech or action is. In these ways students rapidly develop a sense of tone and style, both in speaking and in writing.[68]

Enacting scripts greatly alters the process of creative dramatics; it almost assumes a performer-audience relationship, since the whole purpose of a script is to hold actors to a presumably superior version of the action. A director becomes a part of the process because someone has to make decisions about staging, placement, and movement. Reading becomes part of the dramatic activity, for an actor delivers his lines either by reading them aloud or by reading the lines silently and memorizing them. These elements move the process of creative drama very close to theater as performance, a step which in itself is not necessarily a bad thing, for it brings the two elements of drama into focus for students. And too, it does not mean that the element of freedom, which is the key to creative drama, is gone. But certain restrictions do appear, and for this reason most authorities in the field recommend that the scripted play be used in the secondary classroom and beyond, allowing the lower grades to continue with polished improvisation.[69]

A problem closely associated with scripted drama often finds its way into the regular English classroom where literature is being taught. Frequently the English teacher must deal with plays as formal drama. When this happens, the usual procedure is to assign a play and have the students read it silently. This practice violates the principles of creative drama and the nature of all drama. Plays are action and are meant to be heard and seen; instead of silent reading, drama should be offered for enactment of one type or another. A teacher may give the whole text of a play for homework, but will divide the class into groups responsible for performing a certain portion of the script. In this they may elect their own procedure; perhaps they will wish to update the play and do it in modern language; perhaps they will choose to improvise on the basic ideas within their scene; possibly the emphasis upon character development will be the important element in a scene and students will devise ways to show that emphasis.

For plays of three to five acts, several approaches may be combined: assigned scenes for performed reading; scenes for memorized acting; other scenes for improvisation; and some scenes for listening to recordings of professional productions. In these ways students experience a number of approaches to formal drama and are engaged in activities which call for a variety of skills. Still another possibility is to read the play in class and then enact the drama immediately after; the printed word ties to a physical world this way and helps to sharpen reading comprehension by translating the subject into another medium. Students who improvise, enact, and in other active ways become involved with a text seem to remember more about the work than those students who merely read silently and discuss the text.

A number of experimental programs have attempted to employ drama as a key activity in secondary school programs of study, but few have been thoroughly explored or have taken into consideration the principles of creative drama. One experimental effort that suggests promise for the classroom is Chamber Theatre. Originated by Robert S. Breen of Northwestern University and developed further by Carolyn Fitchett of the Educational Development Corporation, it offers a combination of some aspects of creative drama and some aspects of formal theater. Fitchett explains the Chamber Theatre approach in the following way:

> Chamber Theatre is a technique for dramatizing point of view in narrative fiction. Its use in the classroom is aimed at helping students to become more aware of the controlling intelligence

and the dynamic relationship between him and the characters of a short story or novel. The narrator is encouraged to talk to the audience in a voice from the characters' world and take the audience into that world. He invites them to see for themselves. He also has the freedom to move in time and space. The students are encouraged to study the story or novel for the unique or individual perspective presented.

The observation of brief passages staged in the classroom helps the student to hear, to feel, and see more clearly than he would ordinarily through reading silently—to examine human motivations (the actions of the mind) as well as physical motions (the actions of the body). In addition, the process of working out passages for staging forces the student director to take a closer critical look at the work; not only *what* the narrator says, but also *how* he says it (style). [70]

Although the technique is experimental, the approach demands the kind of thinking and action which encourages students to use their dramatic imaginations as one means for gaining more insight. Students who have experienced creative dramatic activity should find the Chamber Theatre approach a helpful one.

By now it should be apparent that creative dramatics is not confined to a specific age or grade level. Treating each of the aspects of creative drama at each new level is not a waste of time because as students mature they become involved in more complex experiences. Subject areas remain to be explored for new approaches utilizing creative drama. Nevertheless, the older students become, the more difficult it is to introduce them to dramatic work. To break down inhibitions, a great amount of experimentation is called for; unison work, unison acting as the teacher reads the narration, small group charades, crowd scenes with different roles, and rehearsed and unrehearsed readings of short scripts are among the ways to involve students in creative dramatic work.

The approaches outlined in this chapter are important to the success of creative dramatics, but the element which holds all the others together and which must not be overlooked is that of evaluation. The period of evaluation is not a time to criticize directly but rather an opportunity to reflect what the creative activity looks like from the outside and thereby to broaden its range of possibilities. That is why after every creative activity time is taken to let students assess the action. An actor needs to know whether he has succeeded or not, and it is the group's responsibility to let individuals know where they were strong and where they might improve. Critical perception comes slowly at first. Eventually comments such as "Jean wasn't any good" will, with guidance from the teacher, turn into statements such as "Jean was very believable when she frowned at John, but I wonder if perhaps she could then smile at Joyce to show the contrast in the action more." Given in the right climate and with the proper guidance, constructive comments will suggest alternative behavior; sometimes replaying a scene with exchanges of roles will help in the evaluation. The teacher's role is to ask questions when they are needed to bring spontaneous reactions from the students. Gradually students will accept the responsibility of evaluation themselves, peer criticism being more effective in some cases than that of the teacher.

The teacher who decides to make use of creative dramatic work with his classes does not face an easy task. He must first be prepared to experience suspicion from his students, for they will tend to be wary of anything unusual or new. Administrators will have to encourage teachers to experiment and be willing to accept a certain amount of disturbance before results will begin to show. Diplomacy, desire, and a multitude of teaching skills are demanded, and yet the rewards of seeing students relax, develop new poise, and discover new horizons of learning will spur the teacher on to further experiences. The contagion of spirit which infects students involved in creative dramatic work is the contagion of learning and responding to each other and the world about them. This is what education should be all about.

Notes

1. Way, *Development through Drama*, p. 65.
2. Creber, *Sense and Sensitivity*, p. 97.
3. Borton, *Reach, Touch, and Teach*, pp. 98-99. Copyright © 1970 by McGraw-Hill, Inc. Used with permission.
4. Way, *Development through Drama*, p. 85.
5. Ibid., p. 87.
6. Cole, *The Arts in the Classroom*, p. 70.
7. Slade, *Child Drama*, p. 189. Reprinted by permission of the University of London Press.
8. Moffett, *A Student-Centered Language Arts Curriculum*, p. 38.
9. Ibid., p. 41.
10. Fast, *Body Language*, p. 1.
11. Hall, *The Silent Language*, pp. 163-64. Copyright © 1959 by Edward T. Hall. Reprinted by permission of Doubleday & Company, Inc.
12. Walker, *Eyes on Mime*, p. 12. Formal mime has many branches, each one with its own idiom. The mime of classical ballet is unlike that in plays; silent film mime of the Charlie Chaplin era is different from the technique of theaters of pantomime in France or Denmark, while the Japanese and Chinese have specialized gesture languages of their own. For the purpose of this discussion we will use the terms "mime" and "pantomime" interchangeably in the sense indicated by Walker's definition.
13. Ibid., p. 37. Copyright © 1969 by Kathrine Sorley Walker. Reprinted by permission of The John Day Company, Inc.
14. Loren E. Taylor, *Pantomime and Pantomime Games*, p. 13.
15. Walker, *Eyes on Mime*, p. 83.
16. Osten, "Structure in Creativity," p. 440.
17. Creber, *Sense and Sensitivity*, p. 87.
18. Walker, *Eyes on Mime*, p. 123.

19. Loren E. Taylor, *Pantomime and Pantomime Games*, p. 4.
20. Moffett, *A Student-Centered Language Arts Curriculum*, p. 167.
21. Johnson, "Black Kinesics—Some Non-Verbal Communication Patterns in the Black Culture," p. 18.
22. Ibid., p. 20.
23. See Way, *Development through Drama*, pp. 235-55, for suggestions on how to deal with scenes of conflict and violence.
24. Coggin, *Uses of Drama*, p. 244.
25. Heathcote, "Improvisation," p. 27.
26. Moffett, *Drama: What Is Happening*, p. 28.
27. Sievers, "Creative Dramatics as a Force in Social Adjustment," p. 393.
28. See Morrison and Foster, "The Use of Creative Drama with Children," p. 7. See also Duke, "Livening Up Nonfiction."
29. See Magers, "The Role-playing Technique in Teaching a Novel."
30. Dewey W. Chambers, *Storytelling and Creative Drama*, p. 73. Reprinted by permission of Wm. C. Brown Company, Publishers.
31. Way, *Development through Drama*, pp. 175-76. Reprinted by permission of Longman Group Ltd. and Humanities Press, Inc.
32. Moffett, *Drama: What Is Happening*, p. 24.
33. Ibid., p. 19.
34. See Kaufman, "Improvised Dialogue in the Junior High School."
35. See Blackmur, "Language as Gesture," for valuable insights about the relation between gesture, tone, and language design.
36. Moffett, *A Student-Centered Language Arts Curriculum*, p. 172.
37. Neill, "Each His Own Dramatist: Spontaneous Acting for Children," p. 752. Reproduced from *The Times Educational Supplement* by permission.
38. Grambs, review of Fannie R. Shaftel's *Role Playing for Social Values*, p. 92.
39. Berger, *Invitation to Sociology: A Humanistic Perspective*, p. 94.
40. Corsini, *Role Playing in Psychotherapy*, p. xi.
41. Ibid., pp. 9-10.
42. See Dumas, "Role Playing: Effective Technique in the Teaching of History."
43. Adapted from Munch, "A Sociodramatic Slant to Science Teaching."
44. Shaftel and Shaftel, *Role Playing the Problem Story*, p. 48. Reprinted by permission of the National Conference of Christians and Jews.
45. Ibid., pp. 37-38. Reprinted by permission. The National Education Association has a collection of stories suitable for role playing entitled *Unfinished Stories for Use in the Classroom*.
46. Potter and Andersen, "Role-Playing in Discussion," p. 135. Reprinted by permission of the Wadsworth Publishing Company, Inc.
47. Ibid., p. 136.
48. Chesler and Fox, *Role-Playing Methods in the Classroom*, p. 40.
49. Ibid.
50. Lippitt, "The Auxiliary Chair Technique," pp. 8-23. See also Chesler and Fox, *Role-Playing Methods in the Classroom*, p. 41.
51. Adapted from Chesler and Fox, *Role-Playing Methods in the Classroom*, pp. 47-48.
52. See Bristow, "Sociometry, Sociodrama and the Curriculum," and Haas, "Implications and Recommendations for Educational Practice: Sociodrama in Education."
53. See Fannie R. Shaftel, *Role Playing for Social Values*, and Grambs and Kinney, "Sociodrama in High School Classes."
54. See Greenleaf, "Sociodrama as a Guidance Technique."
55. Shelhammer, "Solving Personal Problems through Socio-drama," p. 505.
56. Borton, *Reach, Touch, and Teach*, p. 73. Copyright © 1970 by McGraw-Hill, Inc. Used with permission.

57. Adapted from Klein, *Role Playing in Leadership Training and Group Problem Solving*, pp. 165-76. Used with permission of the Association Press.
58. McCaslin, *Creative Dramatics in the Classroom*, p. 59. See also Morrison and Foster, "The Use of Creative Drama with Children," pp. 5-6, Loren E. Taylor, *Puppetry, Marionettes and Shadow Plays*, and Nau, "Making Marionettes for the Classroom."
59. See Belo, "Balinese Children's Drawing," for an account of the effects of shadow plays on children.
60. See Morrison and Foster, "The Use of Creative Drama with Chidren," p. 9. See also Traynor, "Who Knows What Lurks in the Heart of an Old Philco."
61. Moffett, *A Student-Centered Language Arts Curriculum*, p. 289.
62. Moreno, *The Theatre of Spontaneity*, p. 49.
63. See Ward, *Playmaking with Children*, pp. 196-97, for examples.
64. Way, *Development through Drama*, p. 209. Reprinted by permission of Longman Group Ltd. and Humanities Press, Inc.
65. Slade, *Child Drama*, p. 66.
66. Ibid., p. 128.
67. Moffett, *A Student-Centered Language Arts Curriculum*, pp. 297-99. Reprinted by permission of Houghton Mifflin Company.
68. Ibid., pp. 286-87.
69. Ibid., p. 285.
70. Fitchett, "An English Unit: Chamber Theatre Technique." Cited in Moffett, *A Student-Centered Language Arts Curriculum*, pp. 490-91.

PART THREE

A Handbook
of Resources

A Handbook of Resources

Although creative drama techniques have been used in British schools for some time, the use of such techniques in American classrooms has been limited, mainly because few teachers are familiar with the ideas behind creative drama. The greatest impetus for the use of creative drama in American schools came from the work of Winifred Ward at Northwestern University during the 1920s and 1930s. Working with students from nearby elementary schools, she developed the concepts of creative dramatics to the point where they embraced all forms of improvised drama.

Initially the concept of creative dramatics met with acceptance in the elementary schools; creative drama was used quite widely on that level until the 1950s, when the general practice waned because of the renewed emphasis upon academic and scientific education. But since the Anglo-American Conference on the Teaching of English, held at Dartmouth College in 1966, teachers, especially those on the secondary level, have been investigating the many possibilities which drama holds for stimulating creative expression.

This handbook, then, has been developed to serve as a resource for the teacher who wishes to incorporate creative drama into his teaching but who may be unfamiliar with some of the techniques and activities which can be used. This handbook is oriented primarily toward the secondary curriculum, since that is where creative drama has yet to be employed on any large scale; however, the majority of the activities within the handbook can be adapted easily to serve on any grade level, elementary through college.

The activities in the handbook have been selected to develop certain general objectives; the teacher, however, may wish to develop his own specific instructional objectives to meet the needs of his classes and individual students.

1. To promote creative expression with particular emphasis upon movement and speech.
2. To creatively exercise the senses and to creatively express emotions.
3. To develop through dramatic play the processes of discussing, responding, evaluating, and interacting.
4. To develop drama as a learning experience for use on all grade levels.

The nature of creative drama calls for the development of a free yet secure and friendly atmosphere. If students are to respond creatively, they must know that there is no immediate threat to their explorations of, and needs for, expression. Consequently, no formal grading apparatus of students' participation and skills appears in the activities. Continuous evaluation is inherent in the process of creative drama; the ongoing discussion of situations and methods of enacting, trying out of roles, and seeing results encourage constructive evaluation by the participants themselves. Students learn to help each other through constructive comment, and in this way each student becomes aware of his progress and can work to develop his abilities at his own pace. Without such an atmosphere, little spontaneous development of skills or freedom of expression will occur. Working with the natural student-centered activities offered here, a teacher should find ample evidence for his own evaluative purposes.

The various activities within this handbook have been grouped around three major emphases—sensory perception, body movement, and improvisation—but some of the activities overlap or can be easily adapted to function in more than one area. This flexibility is intentional. The development of expression in each of the three general areas calls for a synthesis of skills and understanding, and for this reason the teacher should feel free to make his own selection from the activities offered, grouping them to meet the varied needs of his students. No attempt is made to present a graded or structured program of experiences.

Introductory Activities

The effective presentation of any new idea or subject to students is difficult. It is necessary at the outset to involve and interest students and to establish a frame of reference which will serve for developing later activities. The following suggestions offer some approaches which have been successful in introducing creative drama to older students for the first time. For the teacher who is reluctant to involve himself directly in an "acting" situation, discussion on a general plane can be helpful. Straight discussions of drama should be avoided at first; concentrate, instead, on certain aspects of life which may be important to the group. For instance, some of the following questions might be asked:

1. What does the basketball player feel like at the moment in the championship game when, with eight thousand fans watching him, he must take the foul shot that can mean victory for his team?
2. What does the diver feel just before leaving the diving board?
3. What does the baseball player feel when facing an erratic pitcher?
4. What does the inexperienced rider feel when mounting a strange horse for the first time?
5. What does the teenager feel when he is allowed to take the family car alone for the first time?

From the discussion of feeling, a person is only a short step from discussing what an individual does in each of the above situations. Some alternatives for introductory activities include:

1. Select carefully some of the photographs from Edward Steichen's *The Family of Man* (New York: Simon and Schuster, 1955) which seem to convey emotion clearly. Show these to the class and ask them to consider what emotion(s) are being portrayed. Have the students tell which specific details helped them determine the emotion. Have them pay particular attention to body stance and facial expression. If this book is not available, carefully selected pictures from magazines—minus any captions—can be used. Such pictures can be easily converted to slides and projected so that the class can view them together.
2. Use some form of charades as an introduction to movement and communication, gradually emphasizing the need for accurate communication. Book, movie, or song titles may be used as starters, but then single words or actions should be introduced.

3. Divide the class into two groups (if the class is too large for this, make three, but keep them fairly large). Have one group stand in a straight line in front of the other, seated group. Each group looks at the other without talking or laughing. Observe the standing group carefully; when they seem quite uncomfortable (usually evidenced through shifting feet, tightness of neck muscles and posture), introduce a task for them—counting the number of chairs in the room, the number of squares in the ceiling, etc.—but have the seated group continue to look at the standing one. When the standing group appears to have relaxed somewhat, switch the groups and repeat the process. Once this has been accomplished, have the entire class discuss their feelings, the effects of the sudden isolation, the change, if any, when a task is introduced, etc.

This activity not only makes the students aware of themselves as individuals, but it also introduces them to the acting situation and the idea of focus.

The following activities require somewhat more preparation and should not be used unless the teacher feels he can carry the roles through successfully. The activities are, however, highly effective.

1. The teacher enters the classroom, slams the door shut, kicks a wastebasket, throws his books on the desk, snaps a window shade up, goes to the blackboard and begins to write—only to have the chalk break in his hand. In general his activities should denote great anger but no dialogue should be introduced. During this action, though, the teacher should remain aware of the response of his class to his actions, and when he sees that the members of the class are reacting strongly, he should break the mood with a smile or some other means and begin asking students to evaluate the experience. Questions such as, What did you notice first? Why did you react the way you did? How did you feel? How did you know how I felt? How did the class as a whole respond? What was the atmosphere of the room during this activity? might be asked.

The subsequent discussion of the incident should help students become more aware of how emotion is communicated through bodily movement and gesture.

2. The teacher enters the room displaying considerable anger. He immediately accuses a student (who has been prepared in advance) of some vague misdemeanor. The student defends himself vehemently and a short dialogue ensues with the scene terminating when the student is sent to the principal's office by the teacher. Play the scene quickly to deliver maximum impact; at the conclusion of the scene both teacher and student should develop a discussion with the class, perhaps drawing on some of the questions suggested in No. 1 above. (See Bishop, "Thats What Happen," for further details.)

Although the foregoing activities suggest ways to introduce students to some of the characteristics of creative drama, the teacher's best approach is to draw upon the students' interests and abilities and start from there. Some students will have been introduced to creative drama in earlier grades and so may be ready for more complicated activities. But it is helpful to remind all students, regardless of their ability, of the basic components which constitute dramatic activity.

Sensory Perception

One of the major purposes of creative drama is to develop a heightened awareness of surroundings as well as an increased awareness of the self. The activities which follow suggest means for accomplishing some of this awareness.

Listening

A. Using a tape recorder, record some common household sounds or sounds around the school. Play the recording to the class, asking them to identify the sounds. A worthwhile addition to this activity is to ask students to put down three or four words which describe the sound as it is played. Some sounds which provoke considerable interest are those of a dog eating, dial tone on a telephone, an electric mixer, running a thumb across the teeth of a comb, water dripping into a pan. (See Shuman, "Adjectives on Tape.")

B. Have the group sit quietly for a minute, preferably with eyes closed, and listen to the sounds around them. Then discuss the changes in perception with them and the function of hearing: how it affects us emotionally, how it affects our evaluation of incidents and people.

C. Make various sounds—tapping different objects or surfaces, opening drawers, moving objects—and then ask students to identify the sounds while their eyes are closed.

D. Have students work in pairs: one student makes sounds while the other identifies; then they switch roles.

E. Have one student read a story while another student talks to him; later the reader tells what the story was about and the two students check the text for the reader's accuracy. This kind of activity can be used with larger groups—up to seven—as well.

The following listening activities require more concentration and should be attempted only after some introductory work has been done.

A. Ask students to listen to different sounds around them but to identify also the cause of each sound. If the sound is made by a person, try to fill in details: What does the person look like? What is he doing? Why is he associated with the sound?

B. Have students attempt to link more than one sound together; for example, the sound of rustling clothes inside the room related to the sound of steps outside the room.

C. Link one or more sounds to an imaginary situation involving the student—the sound of a clock ticking and the sound of an approaching automobile might suggest expectation.

D. Associate several sounds as if they were part of a television or film soundtrack. Where are you in the story, beginning, middle, or end? What is happening?

E. Select a particular sound and make it extremely personal. It suggests a wish you would like fulfilled—What is that wish?

F. Add an "if" to the sound selection. What if all the clocks in the world stopped? What if one could not use his feet any more? What if there were no more automobiles?

Brian Way in *Development through Drama* suggests that in the early stages of listening activities, the teacher might wish to utilize the fingers or hands to make different levels and types of sound. Such activity is particularly appropriate with younger children as can be seen in the following excerpt from a class.

Teacher: "Listen. What does this make you think of?"
Sound: with flat of hand on desk, a strong continuous time beat.
Class answers: Giant, soldier, big animal.
Teacher: "Listen again. This is what the giant or the soldier or the big animal saw."
Sound: short bursts of scraping sounds with the fingers on the desk.
Class answers: A mouse, an insect, a bush moving. (p. 48.)

Other ways exist for involving students in sound experiences. For instance, by using a story format students develop sounds of their own. For older students it may be necessary to suggest a television or film format as a framework, but the method of controlling and introducing the sounds remains the same. A large arrow cut from tagboard or some other fairly stiff material is shown to the class. The arrow becomes the control for the volume of sound that will be heard. When the arrow points directly downward, there is no sound; when the arrow begins to rise—moved by the teacher—the volume of sound begins to rise as well. Sound volume can be controlled at all times by this device; once students have practiced following the movement of the arrow a few times, few problems arise. Students become aides or sound technicians in telling the story effectively. The following is a short story that will suggest the kind of material which may be used with secondary students and how the sound becomes a part of the narrative.

Story	Sounds
It had been quite a party. Harry was sound asleep on the couch. Outside a stiff northeast wind was blowing against the house. One of the loose window shutters on the back side of the house slapped against the clapboards. Harry slept on, exhausted from his latest attempt to influence his friends. Suddenly the alarm clock on the mantel piece began to ring. It was 9 o'clock in the morning. Then the telephone rang somewhere in the other room. Harry turned over on the couch and then slipped off it onto the floor. His eyes popped open and his arms flailed out in all directions, knocking over a half-filled glass beside the couch. Slowly he pushed himself erect; he stumbled across the room, hitting an end table and knocking an ash tray to the floor; he finally made it into the hall where the phone began to ring once more. Gingerly he lifted the receiver from its cradle and put the instrument to his ear; the dial tone sounded mockingly in his ear. He looked at the receiver for a moment and then placed it back on the cradle. Shaking his head slowly, he made his way to the bathroom. The door stuck as usual and he had to push hard to get it open; the hinges protested, making Harry grab his head as if in pain. Going to the shower, he turned it on. He then climbed into the tub, clothes and all, and let the water cascade over his body. So began another day for Harry Kallerman.	snoring fade wind in wind continued slapping of a shutter alarm ringing phone ringing sound of body hitting floor glass breaking sounds of passage phone ringing dial tone sounds of hinges sound of water fade sound of water down and out

The teacher who has not done work with sound before may be hesitant because of the "noise" involved and the difficulty of retaining control over the volume. The use of the arrow is one method which has worked effectively, and if students understand that they are contributing to the effectiveness of the story by contributing sounds accurately, usually most of the difficulties will be minimized. One should not expect, however, that students will always produce the sounds which seem called for at a particular point. They may imagine some other sound or they may miss the cue in the story. If this happens the teacher should simply go on with the story and when it is completed, review the action and show where other sounds might have been introduced. These sound stories can easily be adapted to work with movement.

Although the previous examples may seem somewhat too simple for secondary students, the teacher with a little imagination will find ways to introduce a variation such as through the television show or the film.

Touch

A. Ask students to clasp their hands in front of them and then look to see whether the right or the left thumb is on top (usually a 50-50 division). Then ask them to reclasp their fingers in an opposite manner so the other thumb is on top. Discuss with them how this feels. The activity can also be done by crossing the arms and then reversing the procedure, or by asking students to write a short sentence, then to switch hands and write the sentence again.

B. Have students either close their eyes or use blindfolds; arrange different objects in front of them and ask each person to touch the various objects and describe what he feels. Objects which have a variety of textures should be used as well as some which are very similar: e.g., potatoes, coconut in the shell, a peeled grape, apples, sandpaper, oranges, pineapple, rice, sugar, salt. Discuss reactions in terms of the problems of perception.

C. Give each student a small paper bag in which there is a common household article. Without looking into the bag, each student should reach in and feel the object; while doing this, he describes to the rest of the class what he is feeling. The student should make no attempt to guess what the object is but should let the class make the identification from his description. If an individual fails to make his description clear to the class, discussion should be centered on what is lacking in the description, or another student might take the same bag and attempt a description.

If there are too many students in the class to make it feasible for each person to do his description orally, a short writing experience could be developed, with each individual writing out his perception. Another method is to pair students and have them identify each other's object.

D. Working in pairs, students lead each other around the room, taking turns at being blind, placing emphasis on letting the "blind" person encounter as many different objects and textures as possible. Eventually, if the space is available, students become skillful enough so they can guide a person just by voice and eventually from a considerable distance.

Sight

Although most activities require sight, it can be helpful to students to spend some time working on their powers of observation. (See Shuman and Sublett, "Home Study as an Aid to Learning.")

A. Ask students to determine how many different colors there are in the room, excluding the colors of people's clothing.
B. Have students examine a small section of a wall, the ceiling, or the floor, and have them describe what they see.
C. Have students in pairs examine and compare the lines in the palms of their hands.
D. Ask students a number of questions which call for a test of observation:
   1. How many windows are there in the room? (to be done without looking around)
   2. What color are the eyes of the person on your left or right?
   3. What color is the hallway outside the room?
   4. How many doors does a person have to go through to get from the room to the outdoors?
   5. What is the number of the room you are in?
   6. How many chairs are there in the room? (no counting)
   7. Where is the nearest fire extinguisher?
   8. Without looking, what is the color of the shoes you are wearing? Your stockings?
E. Arrange a series of objects on a table where students can see them easily. Let the students look for thirty seconds and then have them close their eyes. Rearrange the objects slightly and have the students look again and tell what has been changed. This exercise can be done a number of times with the changes becoming progressively more subtle as students' powers of observation and concentration sharpen. The same exercise can be done in smaller units, using pairs or small groups of students.
F. Show students a picture from a newspaper or magazine for a short time—thirty to sixty seconds—and then have them compile a list of details taken from the picture. Be certain the picture is dramatic, at least at first; the same thing can be done using slides or transparencies.
G. Give each student an object—key, ruler, protractor, block of wood, eraser, ring, etc. Ask each student to devise as many uses as possible for the object; the only restriction is that the basic shape of the object cannot be changed but the object may be enlarged or made smaller. This exercise can be done orally, written, or most effectively through pantomime.

H. Younger children can be given foreign coins and asked to examine them carefully and list as many details as they can which would help to identify the country, or the kind of country that the currency might come from.

Smell and Taste

Although these two senses present some difficulties, the imaginative teacher with a bit of ingenuity will provide some experiences for the students.

A. Begin with real objects—a piece of cowhide, sachet powder, a piece of old wood and a piece of freshly cut wood, driftwood, plants, pebbles—which provide contrasts in scents; have students develop lists of descriptive words for each object.

B. Suggest certain general categories to students and ask them to suggest smells which might be found in these groupings. Some possible classifications include the seashore, industries of different types, the school, the home, etc.

C. Many activities can be carried out by the students themselves. Brian Way in *Development through Drama* pp. 58-63, has some excellent suggestions for activities in the areas of taste and smell.

Movement

A good part of drama is action of various types, so it is important that students become accustomed to the movement of their bodies in space. Many students tend to be inhibited at first when asked to show feelings through bodily movement. The various exercises that appear here are designed to weaken some of this inhibitive reaction and to prepare the way for pantomime and improvisation, both of which draw heavily upon movement.

1. If possible, square off an area, pushing desks, chairs, and tables aside to form an area. Students then take places inside this space and become molecules in action; they move by walking but they may walk at different speeds, bumping off the sides of the area as well as each other. Students must remember that if they are bumped, they must react; for instance, if a fast molecule bumps into a slow one, the latter is propelled in another direction. Variations on this activity may be suggested, such as having each student become a chemical element which is not attracted to any other element; emphasis is thus placed on moving without contact.

2. Instruction in movement should be presented as imaginatively as possible, giving students some task such as picking apples instead of telling them to stretch as high as they can. Mina

Swaminathan in *Drama in Schools,* pp. 38-39, suggests a sequence of movement activity; although suited for young children, modifications can be made for older students. Only movement patterns are offered, so the teacher will have to convert them into activities.

a. Walking and running at different speeds; speed may be gradually increased or decreased, ending in complete stillness, or in definite steps, changing at a given signal. Rhythm may be introduced as well.
b. Changing the direction of movement at a given signal.
c. Moving freely about and, at a signal, freezing into a "statue."
d. Moving along lines or squares on the floor in a definite pattern, or if no such marks are available, moving along a fixed route, perhaps through a series of obstacles.
e. Moving about a room freely and fast, without bumping into each other.
f. Moving through a group of people in the opposite direction to that of the crowd without bumping into people.
g. Moving in particularly limited ways: blindfolded, on tiptoe, silently, with arms stretched as if for balance.
h. Falling in different ways—as if shot, tired, accidentally, slipping, etc.
i. Stretching up high and walking on tiptoe.
j. Crouching as low as possible and crawling through a narrow tunnel.
k. Swaying, tapping, or walking to rhythmic accompaniment.
l. Laughing and crying.
m. Wrestling, fighting, struggling in pairs.
n. Pushing and pressing with force.
o. Jumping, hopping, and leaping to rhythm and in various combinations.
p. Turning, twisting, and contorting the body and limbs.
q. Making wheeling movements with arms or legs.
r. Imaginary sword play.
s. Making sharp and blunt shapes, or hard and soft. Can be done effectively with shadows and silhouettes.
t. Tension and relaxation.

3. Ball activities: Give each student an imaginary ball. Have him explore the different properties of the ball and define what type of ball he has through his movements. How does it bounce? Is it difficult to catch? How would one throw it? What are different ways the ball can be put in motion? After students have had a chance to explore these aspects of the ball, put several students together—best in groups of five or six—and have them exchange the ball, never repeating exactly the same motion. Speed of exchange can be varied—fast, then in slow motion. A variation on this activity is to put students in several groups and tell them to exchange balls with other

members of the group, but that the same kind of ball cannot be used more than once. Students also can work in pairs or small groups to illustrate sports activities which require the use of a ball—tennis, golf, lacrosse, rugby, football, baseball, basketball, ping pong, soccer.

4. Statues: Involve students in a progressive movement of the different parts of the body, starting perhaps with the fingers—move every joint—then the wrists, the elbows, shoulders, neck, head, face, spinal column. After students have been through the sequence once or twice, lead them through again, only this time have them continue to move all parts of the body. Then on signal they are to freeze in whatever position they may be; variations include the ugliest position they can think of, the funniest, the most awkward, etc. Further use of this activity can be developed in making still photographs.

   Groups of students can build statues as well. Each group decides on what their statue will look like; then, using another group as the parts of the statue, they build it. Another variation is for the constructing group to give verbal instructions which the other group then tries to follow.

5. Furniture as obstacles: In limited space, furniture creates a problem; some of the following activities may be used to alleviate part of the crowding problem, but the movement of objects should be an integral part of some drama.

   a. Members of the class are part of a Mission Impossible Force; it is the task of the force to remove a number of highly explosive gases which are in fragile containers, but there is a sensitive monitoring system in the storage room which reacts and sets off an alarm if any loud noise occurs. The team is working against time since their presence has been detected but the enemy forces are still not certain as to the exact location of the force.

   b. Members of the class are participating in a crafts show and each person is engaged in setting up his exhibit in a specified area.

   c. Members of the class have just received word that they have been ordered to leave the country; they have only a few minutes to gather their possessions and get ready to leave; however, the new exiles do not wish to alert their neighbors that departure is imminent.

Most of the previous activities assume considerable space, preferably a large stage or auditorium. Frequently such facilities are not available, and the teacher is faced with using a classroom with very little floor space. Some of the following activities may offer solutions to this problem.

1. Mirroring: Pair students together and designate one of each pair as the initiator of action, the other as the reflector. The

initiator begins some movement which is reflected simultaneously by the other student. Concentration should be placed on the movement, and speech should be discouraged during early attempts. Roles should be exchanged frequently; eventually students should be able to signal the exchange without using verbal means. A number of variations on this exercise are possible; for instance, once students have become familiar with the process, let them begin without anyone being assigned roles. Discuss with them what happens. Who started the movement? Why? Where did the impetus come from? Which is harder, the designated type of mirroring or the free kind? Why? How does one feel emotionally and physically while involved in this activity? Another variation is the triangular mirror; group students in threes, arranging them in the shape of a triangle, about an arm's length apart. Use the same process as in the mirror exercise except that students are to develop a focal point of vision about in the center of the triangle. A delayed mirror may also be used, starting with pairs and working up to five students. One student begins and completes his sequence of movements; the next person attempts to reproduce those movements exactly and then adds a sequence of his own.

This type of exercise develops students' concentration and attention to movement, factors which are later helpful in pantomime and improvisation work. The mirror exercises also function well as warm-up activities.

2. Simple movement: Ask students to demonstrate how they would do the following:
   a. eat an ice cream cone
   b. eat cotton candy
   c. eat a hot, toasted marshmallow
   d. eat a boiling-hot ear of corn
   e. walk through deep snow
   f. walk through fallen leaves
   g. walk through a driving rainstorm
   h. walk across a plowed field
   i. walk in a windstorm
   j. walk up and down sand dunes
   k. walk across pebbles in bare feet
   l. walk in high heels
   m. walk in sandals
   n. walk in army boots
   o. walk in slippers
   p. walk with a cast on one foot or leg
   q. touch a hot radiator
   r. handle a handful of dirt
   s. pick up a heavy suitcase.

3. Suggest simple activities which may or may not require more than one person: picking apples that are just out of reach,

loading a car with assorted boxes of different shapes and weights, carrying a heavy piece of furniture such as a refrigerator or a living room couch.

4. Machine exercise: Select one student to start a movement typical of a machine part, such as a piston working up and down or back and forth. One by one other students should join him, each person moving in a way to complement the first student's movement. The exercise works best with five to ten students; a teacher can have several of these groups going at once.

5. Stagecoach: The driver of a stagecoach sits in the center of the circle of students and spins a yarn about a hair-raising ride through the Wild West. He assigns the various parts of the stagecoach to members of the group; the parts may include the wheels, horses, axles, seats, doors, windows, lantern, etc. As he spins his story, the driver will mention the parts; as each one is mentioned, the person assigned that part will try to act it out. The stagecoach should be built and operating before the end of the story. An appropriate way to bring the story to a close is to have the stagecoach meet a perilous end and have all the items fall apart. A possible variation on this exercise can be worked with the "Deacon's One Hoss Shay" by Oliver Wendell Holmes.

6. Basic blind: Sketch a scene location briefly: room, type of furnishings, etc. Establish the what, who, and when of the situation. Blindfold group members. The objective of the exercise is to devise ways in which things may be handled and passed from one person to the next; the occasion might be a party or a shopping trip in a supermarket. Real props are used at first and then later the scene is played without them. Players are to keep moving around the area just as if they could see. It is advisable, however, to let students gain confidence in nonverbal communicative skills before attempting this activity. Play the scene with all boys or all girls before combining the two.

7. Facial movement: Students need practice in emotional expression in nonverbal modes, for communication often relies on the facial expression of the speaker and listener. Students may be given certain emotions such as fear, anger, surprise, joy, ridicule, embarrassment to play out through facial movements. Charles Aubert in *The Art of Pantomime* suggests that instinctive expressions have certain general characteristics. Here is how he categorizes them:

"All expressions which are stamped by will and intelligence in whatever degree, such as covetousness, anxiety, reflection, intellectual effort, scorn, disgust, horror, anger, defiance, combativeness, bravery, pride, struggle . . . etc., are always characterized by drawing the eyebrows down and together, forming at the base of the forehead vertical wrinkles, and are also accompanied by a tension of the limbs and whole body.

"Expressions where intelligence and will are inactive for the moment, such as hesitation, ignorance, admiration, stupefaction, fear, extreme physical suffering, gayety, laughter, enjoyment and petulance are always characterized by extreme elevation of the eyebrows which causes horizontal lines on the forehead. They are accompanied also by relaxation of the muscles and flexion of the limbs.

"Some of these emotions may be experienced, those for instance against which it would be useful to react, such as anxiety, fear, physical suffering—while still retaining to a certain point the will to struggle. In this case cross lines are formed on the forehead; that is, the vertical lines persist in spite of the predominance of horizontal lines. But when these emotions, gaining greater intensity, entirely paralyze intelligence and will, the vertical lines completely disappear. All the expressions which indicate a resolve, an activity or a charm, such as: to admire, desire, pray, persuade, order, threaten, brave, etc., require that the weight of the whole body be carried on the forward leg, and the head held erect.

"On the contrary, all expressions which portray indecision, timidity, or dislike, such as to hesitate, doubt, meditate, be frightened, scorn, dread, etc., are completed by throwing the weight of the body onto the backward leg. All expressions of intense emotion impel the raising of the shoulders." (p. 7.)

Although the teacher will not introduce students to a technical discussion such as Aubert's, he can, through certain activities, bring students to realize that many of the signs which Aubert suggests are a part of communication. For instance, ask students to perform the following:

1. In how many ways can surprise be shown? Examples might be the arrival of an unexpected guest, an unexpected scolding, the failure of a test that was assumed to be easy, discovery of a mouse under your chair.

2. Situations: You receive a telephone call from your date for the evening; he can't take you to the dance; show your reaction.

   or

   You have just received a telephone call from the police station—your son has been in a serious accident.

   or

   You have just been notified that you have received first prize in some contest; the prize is an all-expense-paid trip to Paris.

3. Progressive emotion: In this exercise the teacher engages in what is called "side-coaching." Tell students the details of a situation and as each detail is offered, have students attempt to portray the different reactions called for. As an example:

someone has just insulted you; you resent this—your resentment grows to anger and the change of feeling becomes evident in your face; then, as the anger becomes uncontrollable, you are moved to strike at something.

4. Other emotional stimuli:
   a. Listen to a joke as if you are rather deaf; try to show your confusion and uncertainty through facial expression as you attempt to discern the point of the story; finish by laughing to avoid embarrassment.
   b. Tell students the next time they find themselves in a conversation which is not particularly interesting to do some of the following:
      (1) Show no emotion—vocally or facially—while the other person is talking to you; just stare blankly at him while he's talking.
      (2) Keep looking bewildered while he's talking; pretend with your face that he is speaking a language you don't understand.
      (3) Laugh, look disappointed, pretend astonishment, when what the speaker is saying calls for no such reaction. For example, if the person is telling a joke, react as though he just announced the doubling of your income tax; if he's telling you a recipe, pretend he's just told you a joke to end all jokes; if he's telling you about the party he went to last night, pretend he's telling you the solution to a difficult math problem and you can't quite follow; if he's telling you about a new car or new clothes, act as though he is telling you about the death of his pet dog.
      (4) Over the telephone—don't say anything that shows approval or disapproval or interest or amusement. Just say "oh" whenever you feel the speaker wants you to say something. Warning: let the victim in on the joke some time before he assaults you. (From Friedrich and Kuester, *It's Mine and I'll Write It That Way*, p. 59. Used by permission of Random House, Inc.)
   c. How many different ways may hot or cold be shown? For example, burning one's hand on a hot stove, holding an ice cube in your hand or mouth, walking in the hot sun, in the cold wind. This type of exercise brings in emotional reaction and body movement; it can be a problem situation as well—how would one show the difference between hot and cold water coming out of a faucet?
   d. Grope your way through a dark and dangerous passageway which has a roof so low that it is impossible to stand upright; see a faint light at the end of the passageway and make your way toward it. Come out into the daylight; be struck by the blinding change in light and fall to the ground dazed and blinded (a good activity for progressive coaching).

Pantomime

It is a common misconception that pantomime is merely a way of doing without words. Actually, pantomime is more like thinking overheard, for it begins and ends before words have formed themselves. Pantomime also illustrates that drama comes from within; the pantomimist who plays his role well is the one who through the power of movement is able to communicate his ideas and inner emotions to others. For this reason the introduction of pantomime is an essential step in the development of creative dramatics. Although some of the previous activities have suggested pantomime activity, the following exercises will be useful in introducing students to more concentrated work in the area.

1. Action pantomime for focus. Students decide upon some activity and then each does it in his own way; some possible choices include washing clothes, sharpening a pencil, digging a hole, riding a bicycle, reading a newspaper, cutting down a tree. Much of this work can be done in small groups with members taking turns, or it can be done all at the same time. Other simple pantomimes include:
   a. brushing one's teeth
   b. washing one's face
   c. nailing two boards together
   d. putting on a pullover sweater
   e. putting on heavy shoes or boots
   f. doing the dishes
   g. fixing a flat tire
   h. using a vacuum cleaner
   i. using a broom or a shovel or a hammer.

2. Sometimes students are interested in classical pantomime, most frequently found in ballet. The simple gestures which form the vocabulary of pantomime can be compared to everyday situations where gestures are used in communication.

A Vocabulary of Pantomime:

Identify oneself: pointing to oneself with the right forefinger.
How one is dressed: a sweeping gesture with both hands inward and then outward, from shoulder to hip.
Love: hands upturned and crossed at the wrists in front of the heart.
Beautiful: right hand, with thumb next to face, describing a circle around the face from right to left.
A kiss: touching the lips with right forefinger.
Table: hands, palms downward, crossed in front of the body and then moved apart to each side.
Drink: pouring from an invisible container with the right hand,

raising the hand, fist clenched but thumb pointing to mouth, and tipping the head slightly back.

A question: hands upturned in inquiry.

Dancing: arms raised high above the head and hands circling each other.

Death: hands over head and then plunging, crossed, downward in very violent movement.

Marriage: the "me" gesture and pointing at third finger of left hand with right forefinger.

Swearing a pledge: the first two fingers on the right hand, raised and turned outward, with the arm up.

To beg or plead: hands clasped and raised with arms bent at the elbows.

Flight: a sweeping up-and-down arm gesture.

Mother: arms crossed over the breast in a centralized position.

Sleep: head resting with eyes closed, sideways on the fingers of the left hand which are laid in the palm of the right hand.

3. Object involvement: Give students such objects as chairs, books, coat hangers, pieces of paper, articles of clothing. Individually or in groups the students are to form a meaningful pantomime using as many of the objects as possible. The emphasis here is not so much upon what is being done but rather with the imaginative uses to which each article may be put.

4. Present students with an imaginary box and place it where all can "see" it. Ask someone to open the box, which is tied securely, and then remove one object from it; the remainder of the group attempts to identify the article from the way it is handled; large or small groups may do this and the activity can become more complex by having each article passed around the group, thus causing each person to respond imaginatively through direct action.

More complex pantomime activity and skills are called for in the following exercises:

1. While one student works out a particular pantomime, ask another student to approach and join the activity; for instance, one student may be attempting to lift a heavy piece of furniture; another student may join him and together they define the spatial and movement problems and carry them to a successful resolution.

2. The staging of a mock battle may be used to emphasize coordination of movement; a variety of imaginary weapons can be introduced to vary the responses; teachers hesitant about engaging students in "battle oriented" action should consult pp. 235-55 in Brian Way's *Development through Drama* for a convincing rationale.

3. Occupational mime: These mimes may include any actions which are likely to take place in an office, factory, store,

home, etc. The mimes may be broken into specific scenes such as a nurse and a patient, a barber and a customer.

4. Let students pantomime the meanings of a pair of words which have the same spelling and/or the same sound but different meanings, e.g., dye and die; piece and peace.

5. Character mime: Establish a simple setting such as a bus stop, railroad station, etc. Ask for volunteers to show people of different ages. The student writes the age of the person to be portrayed on a slip of paper which he gives to the teacher; then the student demonstrates how a character of that age might act in the provided environment; evaluation by other group members determines his success; the exercise may be done many times with emphasis placed on different character traits.

6. Camera: Let a student begin some activity in pantomime. Another student becomes a cameraman who is recording the action; the cameraman moves around adjusting the movement, taking long shots, close-ups, medium shots, wide angles, special perspectives, etc. Roles can be exchanged and played again.

Eventually students will wish to develop more involved pantomime which shows a sequence of events or the development of a story. Here are some suggestions for starters in such activity.

1. Three teammates are arguing with an umpire over a bad call in a close baseball game.

2. You have a blister on your heel which is very painful; you know that you are late for school and you are only halfway there; show what you would do.

3. Set a group scene, perhaps a busy intersection in a city. Suddenly there is an automobile accident; have each student relate to the accident and through mime indicate who he is, what he is doing, how he relates to others around him, his reaction to the accident. The activity can be done many times with varied settings and situations.

4. Watch as an airplane taxis onto a runway and prepares for departure; someone you care for very much is on the plane and this is the last time you will see that person. Watch the plane as it takes off and disappears toward the horizon. Additional details such as standing on a windy observation deck or standing in the midst of a crowd may be added for increased complexity. Side coaching is possible here.

5. You are a burglar picking the lock on a safe; you hear something and turn to find yourself facing a policeman, the owner of the house, a little baby, a dog. What do you do?

6. Ask students to respond to this situation: You are going fishing and are in a boat on a large pond; taking your fish pole, you bait the hook and then put the line into the water; after a

time you get more and more impatient; suddenly you feel a bite; you hook a fish and play him; finally you are able to reel him into the boat; it is the largest fish you have ever caught.

7. Animal mime: Each student becomes a particular animal and creates a pantomime situation of either a serious or humorous nature. Students may wish to mime a human situation through the use of animals.

8. Give two students different descriptions of the situation they will be acting out. For instance, tell one student that he is in a lifeboat on the ocean after two weeks at sea and he is delirious from drinking too much salt water; he is trying to get his partner to signal a plane flying overhead. Tell the second student that he is in a bathtub taking a bath. While there, he is interrupted by a drunk.

Dialogue

It usually does not take much urging for students to develop dialogue from pantomime activity. Although a certain amount of straight pantomiming is desirable in the beginning, spontaneous dialogue should be encouraged gradually as students become more involved in complex situations. Many of the exercises which have been offered in the pantomime section lend themselves naturally to dialogue, and students undoubtedly will wish to return to them for that purpose. Some of the following activities, however, offer a bridge to the use of speech with dramatic action.

1. Give students different words to portray, such as "love," "anger," "sorrow," etc. All the portrayals must be done without using words; in place of conventional words, students are to use letters or numbers to convey the proper emotion; emphasis in communication is thus thrown onto intonation and facial and physical movement.

2. Set a scene which allows for the introduction of several characters; for instance, a man is painting his house; a woman enters and must relate to the painting activity and establish her relationship to the painter; others should join gradually and do the same. This can be done in mime alone and then with dialogue. If the class is too large for everyone to participate, some class members could write a short account of what happens, and these could later be used as a basis for evaluation.

3. Tell students that they are immigrants on a ship which has just arrived in a foreign country; the immigrants have severed all ties with their homeland and can never return. The students acting as the immigrants are to convince customs officials that this country should allow them to enter and settle. To add to

the development of the scene, it might be played in the following sequence:

a. using only pantomime
b. using pantomime and nonsense words
c. using pantomime and spontaneous dialogue.

4. Given a situation such as a confrontation between a policeman and a motorist, have students enact a scene in which they communicate only by humming or by using a musical instrument such as a kazoo; all attempts should be made to play the scene as if regular dialogue were used. The scenes are effective played first with the nonsense speech and then regular dialogue. Other situations include a patient attempting to explain an illness to a doctor, a motorist attempting to explain a problem with his automobile to a mechanic.

Improvisation

With the introduction of pantomime and dialogue, students move naturally to the next level of creative dramatics, which is improvisation. The emphasis in this aspect falls upon student-initiated activities and interpretation as well as upon the skills of communication. At first it may be necessary for the teacher to introduce various scenes or situations and to sketch the background simply, and even, if necessary, indicate certain character roles. Students should be encouraged to give free rein to their imaginations. The following activities act as improvisational starters. Many call for role playing a type, but role-playing situations in general will be discussed later in this section.

1. Problem situations for improvisation: Provide students with minimal situations and character identities and then ask them to develop spontaneous interpretations.

a. Take home a bad report card and present it to your father and mother, who are very grade conscious.
b. You are a traveler who has lost his ticket and you are trying to explain the situation to an unfriendly conductor.
c. You are a bad-tempered man buying from a deaf store clerk.
d. You are a timid person talking to an aggressive car salesman.
e. Argue with a brother or sister over who gets to use the family car.
f. Argue with a brother or sister over which television program to watch.
g. You are a salesman on the first day of the job, trying to sell a product to a housewife.
h. You must tell your father that you have just been arrested

for speeding or that you have had an accident with the family's new car.

i. You want to tell your boyfriend or girlfriend that you don't want to go steady anymore.

j. A good friend has asked you to go to the drive-in; your mother says you must stay home and do your studying; you don't want to hurt your friend who has been asking you for a long time to go with him, but your mother is standing near enough to hear what you are going to do.

k. Discuss with your husband or wife the rearrangement of furniture.

l. Complain to your son or daughter about the condition of his or her room; or react to your mother's complaints about your own room.

m. The sun and the wind are having an argument over who is more powerful; play to some resolution.

2. Occasionally ask students to exchange roles on signal; that is, a young person might suddenly have to adjust to being an older person in the middle of the dialogue. Attempts should be made to keep the action flowing as smoothly as possible during the switch.

3. Record a soap opera episode. Play the tape to the climactic point; stop the tape there and have students choose roles and improvise an ending. Compare/contrast with the original.

4. Introduce the newspaper as a possible source for potential drama; let students select events which they feel contain the necessary elements for convincing drama. Then have students work out their own interpretations of the news. (See McCarroll and Poley, "All the News and No Print: An Adaptation of the Living Newspaper," and Perry, "Living Newspaper.")

5. Use poems and short stories as improvisation starters; selections should be made carefully, though, to insure dramatic involvement. Poems or stories that rely heavily on natural description will be difficult to enact. However, works which involve clear conflict and have a strong narrative line will usually play well (see suggested listing later in this handbook). Folk ballads, dramatic monologues such as "My Last Duchess," stories which use mystery such as "Cask of Amontillado," and excerpts from novels are possible materials. The teacher may read only the first part of the story leading to the climax and then let students improvise their interpretations of the ending; another method is to sketch the setting, characters, and conflict of a work and then let the students improvise from there. Still another variation would be to discuss thoroughly the work and then establish a hypothetical situation in which the characters of the story operate. With poems it sometimes is helpful to read the work orally several times to be certain students "see" the poem; then it may be mimed as the poem is read, or it may be freely adapted without reading.

6. Lifeboat: There are ten (more or less) people on a lifeboat, but room, food, and provisions for only four people are available. The group must decide who stays and who is to be sacrificed. Initially it may be helpful to assign character roles such as an elderly man, a young child, an expectant mother, a sailor, a millionaire. Students must come up with reasons for their choices and present them to the class for decision. A variation on this activity is to establish the setting in a bomb shelter with similar restrictions. (See Leo J. Schools, "Lifeboat.")

7. Dialects: Students in language study often become interested in the various dialects which can be found in their own geographical area as well as those found in other parts of the world. The following are situations which call for this kind of awareness:

a. Two gangsters discussing the effect on their actions of recent police investigations.

b. Two Yankees discussing the effects of the weather on crops.

c. Two Southerners discussing the weather.

d. Two Englishmen commenting upon sights in America.

Combinations where two distinct dialects are called for within a situation often prove interesting; the use of dialect passages from Mark Twain and Marjorie Rawlings is a good device as well.

8. Beginnings and endings: As students become more accustomed to improvisation give them beginnings and endings to situations and ask them to expand them into recognizable form.

a. A group of people waiting in a room for: a telephone call, the arrival of someone, a telegram, one of them to make a decision.

b. Sentences: "I thought they were coming." "No one knows what happened but...." "We're ready to go now." "Wait five minutes and then follow." "Who are those people watching us?"

9. Skeletal situations: Establish situations which can have many variations and which call for a large number of roles. For instance, develop a setting in which people are standing in line—perhaps a ticket line at a theater, a checkout line at a grocery store—and then introduce some kind of conflict—a robber, a fainting person, etc., and let students identify their own roles and resolution.

Role Playing

As was indicated earlier, all dramatic situations call for a type of role playing; however, in some instances more emphasis is placed on the role itself and its characteristics than on the other dramatic conventions involved. The following items suggest possible focusing situations where roles are central to playing out a situation. Great care should be exercised to allow ample time for discussion and evaluation once the role playing has been completed so that a separation between role and reality may occur. Failure to do this often causes discipline and emotional problems. Sociodrama, a form of role playing, is included in the suggested situations given here, but it is not labeled separately. In most instances, role playing is effective when based on real situations closely related to the students' background; for this reason the teacher may find that he will need to adapt some of the following suggestions in order to tailor the situations to his classes.

1. The school day has just ended; everyone has left the classroom except the teacher and two students; the teacher is making last minute preparations to leave and is in a hurry since he has a meeting to attend in a few minutes. John, one of the students, has been working up his courage for three days to speak to the teacher about a grade he received on a paper; he feels he has to ask now or his courage will leave him. Sue, the other student, has a note from her mother that was supposed to be given to the teacher and requires an answer; Sue had forgotten to give the note to the teacher and knows that her mother will be angry if she comes home without an answer.

2. Jack is an extremely talented actor; he has been selected to play the part of a female in a Shakespearian play the school is producing. Some of the other students are making remarks about his playing the part and Jack does not know what to do. Possible scenes:
   a. Jack and the guidance counselor
   b. Jack at play rehearsal
   c. Jack and a group of boys in the hall.

3. A student is walking down the street and ahead of him two large boys are beating a smaller boy; as the student comes nearer the little boy calls for help; the bigger boys tell the approaching student to mind his own business.

4. Three people have been assigned a project. Two of the students are excited about the idea and have many plans; the third student is not interested and criticizes all the ideas. The project is going nowhere and the time for it to be done is only a few days away.

5. A student is late finishing his work in class, but the person in front of him has finished and keeps interrupting.

6. The teacher has asked the class for criticism about the way the class work is proceeding; several students have some ideas about how the work could be made more interesting but they

hesitate to suggest anything because they are afraid the teacher will not accept the ideas.

7. A classmate always hits everyone he sees. He claims it is his way of saying hello, but students are getting tired of having black and blue marks all the time from where he has hit them.

8. A new student has entered the class, and he has a different speech dialect from the rest of the class. Some students make fun of his speech and the new student is obviously ill at ease.

9. A student's parents tell him that they do not approve of some of his friends. He likes these people and feels that their influence is not harmful; he tries to convince his parents of this.

10. A young boy of about fourteen in accused of stealing; he is in court with his mother, a lawyer, the arresting officer, the judge, and the prosecuting lawyer. Act out the situation.

11. High school dress regulations say that skirts may not be more than an inch above the knee. A student is wearing a skirt that is three inches above the knee and the principal has stopped her in the hall and has asked her about the length of the skirt. A crowd of other students has gathered.

12. Some neighborhood parents are asking that more ethnic literature and study be introduced into the curriculum. Enact a meeting between these parents, the principal, some teachers, and the superintendent.

Scripted Drama

Students often progress in their dramatic work to the point where they wish to develop scripted plays. This aspect of drama can be introduced in several ways.

1. Give each student the opportunity to write a single, uninterrupted scene which is playable in five minutes and is limited to two characters. No directions should be given to students about the need for conflict, stage directions, etc. Once the scenes have been written have them discussed and tried out in groups. Let students edit as much as they wish, for out of the necessary discussion should come some of the characteristics needed for effective drama. Let the groups continue working on the scripts until they have what they consider a satisfactory product. Then have the scripts exchanged among groups and tested by playing.

2. For students who are not familiar with writing dialogue, collect a number of pictures which show expressive faces, and mount two pictures facing each other on a sheet of paper. Have the students create a short speech for each character shown or just one speech directed from one person to the other.

3. Another role playing starter as well as stimulus for script-writing is to select pictures without captions and ask students to identify with the pictured characters and play out what they think is happening. Dialogue from this can be written down and a playlet constructed.

4. Students may want to put into written form some of the pantomimes and improvisational sketches they have worked with previously. This would be a good way to build a classroom library of short scenes to be used with future classes.

5. Students may find that they wish to develop scripted plays based on their reading in subject areas or in familiar books and stories; even comic books and comic strips become potential sources for drama.

A Word about Outside Activities

The major emphasis in this handbook has been upon student participation, with most of the involvement occuring in the classroom during regular classes. The teacher may wish, however, to assign some activities for outside preparation or to offer extracurricular opportunities to students. Usually assignments will be made for the purpose of obtaining additional ideas or background for classroom exercises. Some of the following ideas will serve as guides.

1. Ask students to watch a television show for fifteen minutes without listening to the sound; they should report their reactions and be prepared to discuss the problems and changes which grew out of this kind of activity. Students who do not have access to television might be asked to place their hands over their ears for a short time and observe different members of their family. A variation on this approach is to ask students to listen only to the sound and not look at the picture. Comparison of the two activities is profitable.

2. Students could help collect pictures which show varying emotions or situations good for improvisation.

3. Short pantomime exercises could be prepared outside of class and then presented; in most cases, however, such preparation should be kept to the minimum and the emphasis placed instead on spontaneous portrayal.

4. Students may be asked to watch performances of such groups as the Ace Trucking Company, the Good Humor Company, the Black Light Theatre of Prague, and the National Theater of the Deaf. All of these groups appear on television and offer material and techniques which will interest students.

5. If the school has a drama club, members of the club could perform a scene for a class. Discussion should center around

the differences of interpretation and comparison/contrast of the performance with improvisations done in the classroom.

6. If the local area has a strong theater group, perhaps one with some professional theater people, the teacher can ask some of them to join the class for a discussion about the emotional and communicative aspects of drama.

7. Films which emphasize pantomime and improvisation are good starters for discussion of techniques as well as sources for ideas to be explored in dramatic activity. Such films are usually short and inexpensive; see the filmography in this handbook.

8. Publishers are making available more and more games which involve role playing and creative drama; suggested titles are in the bibliography of simulations in this handbook.

9. Marcel Marceau, renowned French mime, talks about mime on record: *The Mime Speaks Out,* Caedmon Records, Inc., 505 Eighth Ave., New York, New York 10018. Order No. TC 1255, $6.50.

Representative Titles for Dramatic Use

The following titles are merely an indication of the types of literature which may be used for dramatic work; often a work will be used only to provide a skeletal situation or to suggest an idea that may be adapted for other purposes. It should be understood, particularly in reference to the novels, that not the entire work will necessarily be used; frequently only a part of a chapter or a selected episode will be drawn from the work.

Poems:

"Abou Ben Adhem"	Leigh Hunt
"Pied Piper of Hamelin"	Robert Browning
"My Last Duchess"	Robert Browning
"The Highwayman"	Alfred Noyes
"The Devil and the Farmer's Wife"	Anon.
"Get Up and Bar the Door"	Anon.
"The Bat-Poet"	Randall Jarrell
"Home Burial"	Robert Frost
"Mending Wall"	Robert Frost
"West Running Brook"	Robert Frost
"The Witch of Coos"	Robert Frost
"The Death of the Hired Man"	Robert Frost
"Ballad of the Light-Eyed Little Girl"	Gwendolyn Brooks
"She's Leaving Home"	Lennon and McCartney
"West London"	Matthew Arnold
"The Ancient Mariner"	Samuel Coleridge
"Miniver Cheevy"	Edwin Arlington Robinson
"Richard Cory"	Edwin Arlington Robinson

"Mr. Flood's Party"	Edwin Arlington Robinson
"Mamie"	Carl Sandburg
"Fog"	Carl Sandburg
"The Last Leaf"	Oliver Wendell Holmes
"Deacon's One-Hoss Shay"	Oliver Wendell Holmes
"Six Blind Men and an Elephant"	Anon.
"Spoon River Anthology"	Edgar Lee Masters
"The Love Song of J. Alfred Prufrock"	T. S. Eliot
"To His Coy Mistress"	Andrew Marvell
"Naming of Parts"	Henry Reed
"Lord Randall"	Anon.
"The Odyssey"	Homer
"The Iliad"	Homer
"The Congo"	Vachel Lindsay
"The Ballad of the Oysterman"	Oliver Wendell Holmes
"Constantly Risking Absurdity"	Lawrence Ferlinghetti

Novels:

Adventures of Tom Sawyer	Mark Twain
Adventures of Huckleberry Finn	Mark Twain
Homer Price	Robert McCloskey
Captains Courageous	Rudyard Kipling
Robinson Crusoe	Daniel Defoe
Swiss Family Robinson	Johann Wyss
Treasure Island	Robert Louis Stevenson
Shane	Jack Schaefer
Lord of the Flies	William Golding
Bless the Beasts and Children	Glendon Swarthout
Cry, The Beloved Country	Alan Paton
Wind in the Willows	Kenneth Grahame
High Wind in Jamaica	Richard Hughes
A Separate Peace	John Knowles
Of Mice and Men	John Steinbeck
The Red Pony	John Steinbeck
The Pearl	John Steinbeck
Grapes of Wrath	John Steinbeck
When the Legends Die	Hal Borland
The Secret Sharer	Joseph Conrad
The Heart Is a Lonely Hunter	Carson McCullers
To Kill a Mockingbird	Harper Lee
Great Expectations	Charles Dickens
Alas Babylon	Pat Frank
The Yearling	Marjorie Rawlings
On the Beach	Nevil Shute
The Ox-Bow Incident	Walter Van Tilburg Clark
Lilies of the Field	William E. Barrett
Wuthering Heights	Emily Bronte
Mama's Bank Account	Kathryn Forbes
Scarlet Pimpernel	Emmuska Orczy
The Light in the Forest	Conrad Richter

Short Stories:

"Gift of the Magi"	O. Henry
"Ransom of Red Chief"	O. Henry
"Where Love Is, There God Is Also"	Leo Tolstoy
"The Open Boat"	Stephen Crane
"The Bride Comes to Yellow Sky"	Stephen Crane
"The Use of Force"	William Carlos Williams
"Barn Burning"	William Faulkner
"Spotted Horses"	William Faulkner
"The Bet"	Anton Chekhov
"Cask of Amontillado"	Edgar Allan Poe
"The Tell Tale Heart"	Edgar Allan Poe
"The Open Window"	Saki
"A Piece of String"	Guy de Maupassant
"Old Man at the Bridge"	Ernest Hemingway
"The Killers"	Ernest Hemingway
"The Lottery"	Shirley Jackson
"The Man That Corrupted Hadleyburg"	Mark Twain
"The Apostate"	George Milburn
"The Monkey's Paw"	W. H. Jacobs
"The Outcasts of Poker Flats"	Bret Harte
"Adventures of Sherlock Holmes"	A. Conan Doyle

Films

Preservice or Inservice

The following films have been selected to show the kinds of materials which are available for preservice and inservice courses in creative drama. Programs, techniques, and skills comprise the majority of the content.

All That I Am Series   20 min.

This sequence of sixteen films pursues methods of stimulating creativity and skills in all the language and speech arts. The lessons move through discovery of the "inside self"—of memory, imagination, and feeling—to the sensory experiencing of the outside world and expressing the self with others in movement and speech. Individual titles include (1) Who Am I? (2) There Is No One like Me (3) Seeing (4) Listening (5) Listening with the Third Ear (6) Tasting and Smelling (7) Touching (8) Rhythm (9) Movement (10) Voice (11) Darkness (12) Wide Feelings (13) Deep Feelings (14) High Feelings (15) Sounds (16) Pictures.

16mm, b/w. Purchase per title: $100; per series of 16: $1000. Rental per title: $10; per series of 16: $140. Northwestern University Film Library, 1735 Benson Ave., Evanston, Illinois 60201.

The Art of Mime   29 min.

Explores the complexities of the art of mime through the activities of the artist Tony Montanaro. Presents him as a teacher exhibiting the training necessary for mime and his personal views on mime prior to and during the performance itself.

16mm, b/w & color. Rental from Center for Mass Communication, Columbia University Press, 1125 Amsterdam Ave., New York, New York 10025.

Children's Theatre   17 min.

Portrays the activities of the studio theater in Adelaide, Australia, where children study and perform ballet in their own theater. Describes the special training provided to help children understand and interrelate the dance and other arts.

16mm, color. Rental from Australian News and Information Bureau, 636 Fifth Ave., New York, New York 10020.

Come to Your Senses   90 min.

The first part of the film is a documentary of a five-day sensory awareness odyssey at the Big Sur Esalen Institute. In the second segment the film audience is guided through sensitivity training exercises which do not involve touching another person.

16mm, color. Rental from Genesis Films, Ltd., 40 W. 55th St., New York, New York 10019.

Communications Model (English—Fact and Fancy Series)   30 min.

Considers the ways a message is delivered (speech, para-speech, kinesics, writing, and other signaling systems) and the different ways a message can be received or perceived. Explores the role of the perceiver and demonstrates that the efficient message-deliverer must take every possible step to keep the perceiver's attention.

16mm, b/w. Order No. ES-866, Purchase: $125. Rental: $6.75. National Center for School and College Television, Box A, Bloomington, Indiana 47401.

Creative Drama: The First Steps   29 min.

This is an authentic filming of the activities of a group of fourth graders during their first experience with creative drama, developed from the ideas and imaginations of the children themselves.

16mm, color. Purchase: $200. Rental: $15. Northwestern University Film Library, 1735 Benson Ave., Evanston, Illinois 60201.

Creative Dramatics   60 min.

In an informal lecture to a graduate class in Advanced Studies in Teaching Reading and the Language Arts, Professor Wallace Gray of Columbia University focuses on improvisation and involves the students in the kinds of experiences in role playing and imaginative thinking they would offer their pupils in elementary school.

Videotape. Hunter College, Television Center, 695 Park Ave., New York, New York 10021.

Development of Creative Expression through a Study of the Literary Element of Characterization (Enrichment Program for Intellectually Gifted Students)   each lesson 30 min.

Although designed for the education of teachers working with the intellectually gifted, methods and techniques illustrated would be applicable to virtually all teaching situations. Applies J. P. Guilford's "Structure of Intellect" to the development of creative expression and presents the following five lessons: (7) Cognition, (8) Memory, (9) Convergent Thinking, (10) Divergent Thinking, and (11) Evaluation.

Film, b/w. Purchase per lesson: $47.39. Great Plains National ITV Library, Box 880669, Lincoln, Nebraska 68501.

Ghost in the House   35 min.

This presentation of a dramatic production done by class 7-1 at J.H.S. 136 would be of special interest to methods courses in English for high school teachers and general courses dealing with meaningful experiences for ghetto children.

Videotape. Order No. H69P-113. Hunter College, Television Center, 695 Park Ave., New York, New York 10021.

Improvised Drama I   30 min.

Illustrates the aims of the creative drama approach to education with John Hodgson's class of seventeen-year-old boys and Dorothy Heathcote's class of fourteen-year-old boys.

Film, b/w. Purchase: $250. Rental: $30. Time-Life Films, 43 W. 16th St., New York, New York 10011.

Improvised Drama II   30 min.

One group is led into a situation which generates the feeling of revenge in one student; a class in a girls' school studying *Romeo and Juliet* act out Juliet's problem of being secretly married and then betrothed to another; and another class who had been studying the Vietnam War pretends to be working in a rice field in South Vietnam when a Viet Cong agent appears.

Film, b/w. Purchase: $250. Rental: $30. Time-Life Films, 43 W. 16th St., New York, New York 10011.

Improvised Drama in Senior High School

Shows a class of tenth and eleventh graders in one of their first experiences with improvised drama. Ends with comments by the teacher of the class and by another English teacher in the school who had used improvised drama in her literature course.

Videotape. Eugene H. Smith, Dept. of English, University of Washington, Seattle, Washington 98105.

It's Between the Lines: Drama for the Classroom   15 min.

Lessons concentrate on the body and the ways it can be used to express feeling and meaning. Students, mostly middle school, explore and improvise. The effect is one of easy, rough-hewn informality which both describes the rationale behind the course and gives a sense of what actual sessions sound like.

16mm, b/w. Board of Public Education, Parkway, South of 21st St., Philadelphia, Penn. 19103. Purchase from Film Makers of Philadelphia, Inc., 1729 Sampson St., Philadelphia, Penn. 19103.

A Handbook of Resources   149

Just Imagine   15 min.

Students present orientation techniques for developing creative drama by rummaging through an old trunk and creating characterizations based on what they find. Kinescope.

16mm, b/w. Indiana University Audio-Visual Center, Bloomington, Indiana 47401.

A Lesson in Teaching Reading   25 min.

Teacher uses creative play and dramatization of a ghost story to motivate and interest third grade pupils. After understanding the basic story, they learn about consonant sounds of *gh,* antonyms, and words to describe "ghost"; practice silent reading and oral reading; and are assigned independent activities.

16mm, color. Order No. 6049. Purchase: $250. Rental: $9. Universal Education and Visual Arts, 221 Park Ave. South, New York, New York 10003.

A Lot of Undoing to Do   15 min.

Describes an attempt to train teachers in the general philosophy of a process curriculum and then encourages them to generate the specifics themselves.

16mm, b/w. Division of Instructional Materials, Audio-Visual Office, Rm. 328, Board of Public Education, Parkway, South of 21st St., Philadelphia, Pennsylvania 19103.

Movement in Time and Space   30 min.

Promoting activity in drama and dance allows children to "act out" their fantasies and thus to make sense out of experience, and also helps to create a favorable social climate.

Film. Order No. 31432. Rental: $6.10. Pennsylvania State University, Audio-Visual Services, 6 Willard Building, University Park, Pennsylvania 16802.

Mrs. Ryan's Drama Class   35 min.

This film follows the gradual development of a volunteer teacher, a group of elementary children, and a concept of experience they approach together called "creative drama."

Film, b/w. Order No. 101384. Purchase: $240. Rental: $16. Contemporary/McGraw-Hill Films, 828 Custer Ave., Evanston, Illinois 60202.

Roleplaying and Guidance   14 min.

The film treats the use of role playing as a help in solving life problems experienced by a young boy. Shows the boy playing, in turn, the role of his mother, himself, and a school principal. Film demonstrates the usefulness and the ease with which role playing may be used in various school situations.

16mm, b/w. Department of Visual Instruction, University of California, Berkeley, California 94720.

Story Acting Is Fun

Using the fence whitewashing episode from *Tom Sawyer,* the film demonstrates the potentialities of dramatic play as a classroom tool for learning.

Film. Coronet Instructional Films, Coronet Building, Chicago, Illinois 60601.

Creative Drama Starters

The following films have been selected as being representative of the kind of the films available to serve as starters for creative drama activity. Some of the productions use techniques such as pantomime and improvisation; all of the selections, however, should appeal to students' imaginations and should offer them ideas for creative activity.

The Apple   8 min.

A lumpish little man tries vainly to seize the last red apple from a tree. He attempts several schemes but none work. The apple finally is delivered to him; ending provides a surprise. Animated.

16mm, color. Rental from Pyramid Film Producers, Box 1048, Santa Monica, California 90406.

Baggage   22 min.

Throughout the city of San Francisco, a Japanese mime struggles with a piece of baggage—symbolic of her special emotional and psychological burden. She is unable to live with it or without it; only death, in the end, is able to free her.

16mm, b/w. Rental from Pyramid Film Producers, Box 1048, Santa Monica, California 90406.

Bags   10 min.

A sardonic allegory on the nature of tyranny and the twists of revolution. Using animated live objects, the film follows the conflict between a greedy, swaggering bag and miscellaneous attic objects. Suitable for high school and above.

16mm, color. Rental from Pyramid Film Producers, Box 1048, Santa Monica, California 90406.

A Chairy Tale   10 min.

A modern fairy tale of a youth who tries to sit on a chair, but the chair declines to be sat on. Pace is fast and funny; action done in pantomime.

16mm, b/w. Rental from International Film Bureau, 332, S. Michigan Ave., Chicago, Illinois 60604.

The Detached Americans   33 min.

A frank, somewhat brutal look at a core problem in America: the impassive uninterest that Americans have for one another. The film covers a number of the symptoms and causes of the malaise described as "detachment." Excellent stimulus for role play.

16mm, b/w. Rental from Carousel Films, 1501 Broadway, New York, New York 10036.

Exchanges 10 min.

A black man and a white girl meet on a train and fantasize a romantic relationship. Illustrates an experimental psychodrama; for mature high school and college students.

16mm, b/w. Rental from Creative Film Society, 14558 Valerio St., Van Nuys, California 91405.

Family Encounter 7 min.

Seven one-minute vignettes dramatically reveal communication failures in family situations. Excellent for discussion starters and subsequent role playing or improvisation; useful in junior high through high school.

16mm, color. Rental from Franciscan Communication Center, Telekinetics Division, 1229 S. Santee St., Los Angeles, California 90015.

The Fat and the Lean 15 min.

Two disheveled actors, a goat, some furniture, eating utensils, and a few other common objects are the materials; the result is a grimly wry parable on the master-slave relationship. Interesting use of classical mime.

16mm, b/w. Rental from Pyramid Film Producers, Box 1048, Santa Monica, California 90406.

The Hand 19 min.

A stylized and stimulating allegory designed with fine taste; uses the art of puppet animation and two main symbols: a man and a hand.

16mm, color. Rental from Pyramid Film Producers, Box 1048, Santa Monica, California 90406.

The Hat 18 min.

Treats the problem of boundaries and the absurdities which grow out of lines which divide men and nations. Animated.

16mm, color. Rental from Mass Media Ministries, 2116 North Charles St., Baltimore, Maryland 21218.

Have You Heard of the San Francisco Mime Troupe 51 min.

Records in documentary style San Francisco's roving group of troubadours who perform serious and irreverent satirical plays in both theaters and public parks. Records the frustrations, triumphs, and difficulties of developing a theater group that intentionally shocks and offends in a serious attempt to reflect the world. Content is quite mature; should be screened before using in the classroom.

16mm, color. Rental from King Screen Productions, A Division of King Broadcasting Co., 320 Aurora Ave. N., Seattle, Washington 98109.

Incident in a Glassblower's Shop   13 min.

A beautifully photographed but slowly moving psychodrama dealing with the Jekyll/Hyde complex; a glassblower, triggered by the sound of mice in his shop, destroys his creation.

16mm. Rental from Creative Film Society, 14558 Valerio St., Van Nuys, California 91405.

In the Park   15 min.

Marcel Marceau portrays a dozen or more events that may occur during a summer afternoon and evening in a park. His portrayals include expressions of irony, pity, mockery, tenderness, sadness, and joy.

16mm, b/w. Rental from Brandon Films, 221 W. 57th St., New York, New York 10019.

Legend   15 min.

A beauty and the beast tale; story based on a West Coast Indian legend. The feats that the youth must perform to win his fair maiden are distinctly Indian ones, and masks are used in the telling.

16mm, color. Rental from Pyramid Film Producers, Box 1048, Santa Monica, California 90406.

A Man's Hands   5 min.

A witty and fast-cut collection dramatizing the activities made possible by our hands—squeezing, poking, scratching, fixing, zipping, playing, and touching. Provides a helpful perspective for those who are inclined to take a favorite appendage for granted.

16mm, color. Rental from Pyramid Film Producers, Box 1048, Santa Monica, California 90406.

The Mask of Comedy   17 min.

Story of the Commedia dell'Arte, the theater that grew out of the Italian Renaissance, recounted with the help of authentic costumes, traditional masks, historical plates, animation, vignettes from contemporary theater, and marionettes.

16mm, color. Rental from Pizzo Films, 1017 Egret St., Foster City, California 94404.

The Masqueraders   10 min.

Charlie Chaplin, Charlie Chase, and Minta Durfee star in the comic story of a male actor who, after being fired, returns to the movie studio disguised as a woman. A silent film.

16mm, b/w. Rental from Blackhawk Films, Eastern-Phelan Corp., 1235 West 5th St., Davenport, Iowa 52808.

Orfeo   11 min.

The myth of Orpheus and Eurydice told in animation. The lovers play enchantingly together, sometimes merging as one being, sometimes charming the fishes in the water. Then Eurydice disappears; Orpheus travels to Hades where Eurydice is finally returned to him. Fourth grade level.

16mm, color. Rental from Pyramid Film Producers, Box 1048, Santa Monica, California 90406.

Pantomime for the Actor   20 min.

Earl Lewin, pantomime artist, demonstrates the importance of pantomime to the beginning actor. He shows how pantomime can be used to convey emotion, action, character, setting, and plot.

16mm, color & b/w. Rental from S. L. Film Productions, 2872 Partridge Ave., Los Angeles, California 90039.

Parable   22 min.

Presents in pantomime a parable about a white-faced clown who, joining a circus parade, takes upon himself the burdens of the lowly, the abused, and the humiliated. The film is a disturbing one to young people and sparks considerable discussion. The use of the film may be more appropriate for the discussion it evokes than for the display of pantomime.

16mm, color. Rental from Protestant Council of City of New York, 475 Riverside Drive, New York, New York 10027.

The Problem   13 min.

An animated puppet film satirizing the absurdities and dehumanizing effects of bureaucracy. A minor decision (what color to paint the trash box) is passed upward through employees and officers—growing larger in importance—until it reaches the chairman of the board.

16mm, color. Rental from CCM Films, Inc., 866 Third Ave., New York, New York 10022.

The Pusher   17 min.

Tells of an egocentric "pusher" who elbows his way into a job, and then continues to elbow himself on and up until he is elbowed out himself. Pantomimed by actors against a stylized white background.

16mm, b/w. Rental from Brandon Films, 221 W. 57th St., New York, New York 10019.

The Running, Jumping and Standing Still Film   11 min.

An experiment in mimed absurdity; a series of inconsequential adventures. The style of the film is said to lie somewhere between the anarchic surrealism of Dali and the fantasies of Carroll and Lear. Provoking for advanced work in pantomime.

16mm, monochrome. Rental from Pyramid Film Producers, Box 1048, Santa Monica, California 90406.

Sirene   10 min.

A mermaid in a harbor of a surrealistic city is charmed by a young man playing a flute. Thus begins a myth which is a powerful yet somewhat puzzling satire on the bureaucratic entanglements of the judicial process.

16mm, color. Rental from Pyramid Film Producers, Box 1048, Santa Monica, California 90406.

Stringbean   17 min.

A hauntingly wistful story about a woman who cultivates a stringbean plant with tender devotion, revealing how an interior world of strength and beauty copes with a single act of harsh reality.

16mm, color & b/w. Rental from Pyramid Film Producers, Box 1048, Santa Monica, California 90406.

The Toymaker   15 min.

A parable about human relations told through hand puppets. The film illustrates most clearly the tendency of humans to concentrate upon sources of conflict rather than sources of unity. Suitable for elementary through tenth grade.

16mm, color. Rental from Contemporary/McGraw-Hill Films, Princeton Road, Highstown, New Jersey 08520.

Two Men and a Wardrobe   15 min.

A fantasy-parable that concerns the cost of private lives in a modern world; very effective action which provokes considerable discussion.

16mm, b/w. Rental from Pyramid Film Producers, Box 1048, Santa Monica, California 90406.

Unfinished Stories

A series of short films which depict conflicts of conscience and then leave it up to the audience to decide what should be done. The attention to the difference between knowing what should be done and actually doing it makes these films valuable improvisational and discussion starters. Suitable for elementary through 9th or 10th grade.

16mm, color. Rental from Doubleday and Company, Inc., Garden City, New York 11530.

Why Man Creates   25 min.

A series of explorations, episodes, and comments on creativity which probe for the answer to the question why man does create. An excellent discussion starter.

16mm, color. Rental from Pyramid Film Producers, Box 1048, Santa Monica, California 90406.

Simulations

The following simulations call for actual role playing; students are asked to take on identities and to project actions. Teachers should be alert to the confusion of roles and reality and make ample allowance for full discussion of the results from these games.

Body Talk (Psychology Today Games, Del Mar, California 92014, $5.95).

A game designed to help people communicate more effectively without words and to enable them to more effectively understand the nonverbal communication of others. Players express emotions provided on cards and others must try to accurately determine these emotions. Not as involving as some; can be used on all age levels with as many as 10 players.

Game of Sacrifice (Education Ventures, 209 Court St., Middletown, Connecticut 06457, $4.95).

Players deal with the difficulties of consensus decision-making, conflicts of interest, and value clashes. Scoring system is somewhat weak; however, the idea for simulation is excellent and should provoke considerable discussion. Can be played with as many as 60 people.

Hang Up: The Game of Empathy (Synectics Education System, 121 Brattle St., Cambridge, Massachusetts 02138, $15).

Designed to develop empathetic insights, *Hang Up* is a board game in which participants assume make-believe personalities with hang-ups they must successfully act out in conflict confrontations between their game personality and the Street Situations of the game. Humorous situations are built into the game, as are rules protecting those who are more inhibited about acting out feelings. Has been used in grades three through twelve.

Impact (Instructional Simulations, Inc., 2147 University Ave., St. Paul, Minnesota 55114, $160).

A community simulation involving participants as community members. Each person is supplied with biographical information, memberships in various groups, and differential involvement in selected key community issues. Group members are called upon to solve various predicaments and changes. Game takes 6 to 10 hours and can be used from junior high through adult; 20 to 40 players.

Insight (Games Research, Inc., 48 Wareham St., Boston, Massachusetts 02116, $8).

Each participant examines a series of cards which provide him with choices. (In which of these settings would you be happiest? Which of these books would you take with you to a desert island?) He marks his choices and also predicts the choices of others. The game is useful in helping individuals learn more about themselves, about others, in increasing interpersonal communication. Most important, the game is fun and has a low risk level. Can be used with 2 to 20 players.

Inter-Generation Gap (Western Publishing Co., Inc., School and Library Dept., 850 Third Ave., New York, New York 10022, $15).

Treats the relationship between a parent and an adolescent with respect to five issues important for different reasons to both. Parents compete against parents and children against children to develop the best strategies in their relationships. Suitable for junior high through senior high; can be used with 4 to 10 players. Playing time is ½ to 2 hours.

Life Careers (Western Publishing Co., Inc., School and Library Dept., 850 Third Ave., New York, New York 10022, $35).

Involves certain features of the labor market, the education market, and the marriage market as they now operate in the United States. Players work with a profile of a fictitious person, allotting his time and activities. Can be used from junior high through senior high, with 2 to 20 players. Playing time ranges from 1 to 6 hours.

Sensitivity (Sensitivity Games, Inc., 9 Newbury St., Boston, Massachusetts 02116, $10).

A game of psychodrama or role playing which is designed to help individuals learn more about themselves, how they relate to others, and how they identify with others. Players assume the roles of individuals involved in personal crises and improvise and act out individual responses. Useful with older and more mature adolescents, but teachers might try developing their own versions for younger students.

The Value Game (Herder and Herder, 232 Madison Ave., New York, New York, $7.95 for the game plus $.75 for student readings to accompany the game).

The game consists of ten to twenty situations requiring decisions and is designed to help demonstrate the inadequacy of a moral system which is based on absolute right and wrong. Can be used with 5 to 35 players.

The following games emphasize role taking as opposed to role playing. This means that basically more emphasis is placed on the cognitive aspects of the simulation than on the affective. Such games, however, can be useful in establishing situations which cause discussion and later examination of roles and feelings.

Adventuring (Abt Associates, Inc., 55 Wheeler St., Cambridge, Massachusetts 02138, price n.a.).

This is a historical simulation treating intergenerational status and life chances within English social classes. Using yeoman, gentry, and merchant groups, each sector tries to advance its sociopolitical position by controlling the social order in terms of social class resources. Game is especially suited for history, economics, and political science classes. Suitable for use with junior high on. Playing time is between 2 and 4 hours; will accommodate 16 to 30 players.

Cities Game (The Cities Game, 1330 Camino Del Mar, Del Mar, California 92014, free).

A simulation with objectives based on "money power"; four groups—business, slum dwellers, agitators, and government—devise strategies for control, negotiation, and settlement. Coalitions are encouraged to rebuild the city, but each group also has its individual goals. Business and government are chiefly interested in the monetary gains, while slum dwellers and agitators may riot—which would mean loss of points to everyone. Suitable for junior high through senior high. Can be played by 8 to 30; playing time ranges from 1 to 4 hours.

Compass-Community Priority Assessment Simulation (Instructional Simulations, Inc., 2147 University Ave., St. Paul, Minnesota 55114, price n.a.).

Community simulation focusing upon priority formulation in community life. Persons act as members of key city groups, associations, and as individuals. The objective is to determine the merits of over fifty different action programs. Suitable for junior high through adult. Playing time 7 to 10 hours; can be played by 20 to 80 people.

Community Disaster (Western Publishing Co., Inc., School and Library Dept., 850 Third Ave., New York, New York 10022, $30).

Involves a community hit by a localized natural disaster. Each player tries to dispel his personal anxiety for family members who may be within the stricken area, while at the same time trying to operate his community post which is vital to the community's functioning and eventual recovery from the disaster. Works well with junior high through senior high. Accommodates 6 to 16 players; playing time ranges from 2 to 6 hours.

Consumer (Western Publishing Co., Inc., School and Library Dept., 850 Third Ave., New York, New York 10022, $30).

Involves players in the problems and economics of installment buying. Consumers compete to develop their utility points for specific purchases while attempting to minimize credit charges. Suitable for junior and senior high; 11 to 34 players; time required: 2 to 6 hours.

Crisis (Western Behavioral Science Institute, 1121 Torrey Pines Blvd., La Jolla, California 02037; $35 for a 25-student kit and $50 for a 35-student kit).

Simulation of international conflict in which students form teams of 3 to 6 players to manage the affairs of six fictional nations. The nations, with different strengths and military capacities, are faced with the problem of resolving a tense situation in a mining area of enormous importance to the world. Participants use written communication, debate in the World Organization, and military force to achieve their ends. Suitable for junior high through college; plays in 1 to 3 hours.

Democracy (Western Publishing Co., Inc., School and Library Dept., 850 Third Ave., New York, New York 10022, $6.50).

A composite of eight different units that simulate the legislative process. Players act as representatives, giving speeches and bargaining with other players; object is to pass those issues most important to their constituents and thus get reelected. Suitable for junior high through senior high. Uses 6 to 11 players; time ranges from 30 minutes to 4 hours.

Empire (Educational Services, Inc., 15 Mifflin Place, Cambridge, Massachusetts 02138, price n.a.).

Historical learning simulation based on mercantilism and the economic system that evolved during the emergence of the British

Empire. Trade, colonies, charters, government, and British political history provide the scenario and background for interaction. Suitable for junior high through senior high. Uses 16 to 30 players; playing time takes one to two days.

Ghetto (Western Publishing Co., Inc., School and Library Dept., 850 Third Ave., New York, New York 10022, $20).

Deals with pressures that the urban poor live under and the choices that face them as they seek to improve their life situations. Each player is given a fictional personal profile. He allocates his time among several alternatives: work, school, hustling (crime), passing time, and neighborhood improvement. Players learn among other things how neighborhood conditions affect them individually and how such conditions might be improved. Good for junior through senior high. Accommodates 7 to 10 players; playing time is 1 to 3 hours.

Kolkhoz (Board of Cooperative Educational Service, 845 Fox Meadow Road, Yorktown Heights, New York 10598, price n.a.).

Based on the Russian collective farm system and its economic role within the Soviet Union. Student participants engage in role-playing behavior such as that of the State Bank, peasant family member, etc. Has been used from elementary through junior high; takes 2 to 4 hours to play.

Labor vs. Management (Published in *Social Education,* October 1966, price n.a.).

Treats an environment of a labor-management dispute. Each participant is given a background for himself and his community and then must interact with others to improve the relations between the disagreeing factions. Suitable for junior through senior high. Plays in 2 to 6 hours; can use 15 to 30 players.

Napoli (Western Behavioral Science Institute, 1121 Torrey Pines Blvd., La Jolla, California 02037; $35 for a 25-student kit and $50 for a 35-student kit).

Simulation in which participants serve as members of a legislature representing one of two political parties and one of eight geographical regions. The goal of each participant is to be reelected at the end of the simulation by working toward the passage or defeat of eleven legislative bills. Junior high through senior high. Plays in 3 to 6 hours and can accommodate 16 to 32 players.

SIMSOC—Simulated Society (Free Press, 866 Third Ave., New York, New York 10022, $3.95).

Participants act as citizens of a simulated society and treat questions and problems of creating and maintaining social order. Conflicts, social control, defiance, and predicament are central factors. Senior high through adult. Playing time: 1 to 5 hours; accommodates 20 to 30 players.

Recommended Reading for Teachers of Creative Drama

Aubert, Charles. *The Art of Pantomime.* New York: Henry Holt and Company, 1927.

An extremely interesting discussion of the techniques of mime; the text is well illustrated with line drawings showing the different body positions and facial movements which form an integral part of mime. Emphasis tends to be on formal mime, but the material can easily be adapted.

Barnes, Douglas, ed. *Drama in the English Classroom.* Urbana, Illinois: National Council of Teachers of English, 1968.

Emphasis is placed slightly more on regular drama than on creative dramatic activities, but the rationales offered and the extensive bibliography should prove helpful to those teachers who are looking for ways to integrate creative drama with the regular drama program in the high school.

Chambers, Dewey W. *Storytelling and Creative Drama.* Dubuque, Iowa: Wm. C. Brown Company, Publishers, 1970.

Primary focus is on the elementary school. Transcripts of classroom storytelling sessions are offered and are valuable for showing the different ways creative drama situations may be worked out by the students. Extremely helpful for those who are at a loss as to where to begin.

Cullum, Albert. *Push Back the Desks.* New York: Citation Press, 1967.

Filled with activities for elementary and junior high students; uses an anecdotal approach and offers some very helpful ways for integrating creative drama into the regular subject curriculum.

Klein, Alan F. *Role Playing in Leadership Training and Group Problem Solving.* New York: The Association Press, 1956.

Although this book was written with the business community in mind, it contains one of the clearest explanations of role playing. Procedures and problems are considered quite carefully, and some of the role playing situations could be quite appropriate for high school and college.

McCaslin, Nellie. *Creative Dramatics in the Classroom.* New York: David McKay Company, 1968.

A compact overview of dramatics for children; discusses oral speaking and the use of story materials in quite detailed fashion. A good source to begin with. Available in paperback.

McIntyre, Barbara M. *Informal Dramatics: A Language Arts Activity for the Special Pupil.* Pittsburgh: Stanwix House, 1963.

A very valuable source because it is one of the few texts available that treats the use of creative dramatics with the handicapped and remedial students. Emphasis is placed on activities.

Moffett, James. *Drama: What Is Happening.* Urbana, Illinois: National Council of Teachers of English, 1967.

A short monograph which presents some provocative ideas about the placement of drama in the curriculum. Moffett presents a persuasive argument for considering drama as a focal point in students' development. Available in paperback.

_____. *A Student-Centered Language Arts Curriculum, Grades K-13: A Handbook for Teachers.* Boston: Houghton Mifflin Company, 1968, 1973.

One of the foremost spokesmen for the use of drama as a central aspect of the curriculum, Moffett offers a number of ways for the classroom teacher to introduce drama into all aspects of English. The book is filled with student examples and activities. The text is particularly valuable because it offers a sequential development of skills and knowledge from K to 13.

Sayre, Gwenda. *Creative Miming.* London: Herbert Jenkins, 1959.

A somewhat technical explanation of mime, but the book contains valuable activities for teaching mime to students.

Siks, Geraldine Brain. *Creative Dramatics: An Art for Children.* New York: Harper and Brothers, 1958.

One of the best texts in the field. Treats fundamental principles of creative dramatics very clearly and includes suggested teaching materials. Good beginning for the uninitiated.

Siks, Geraldine Brain, and Dunnington, Hazel B., eds. *Children's Theatre and Creative Dramatics.* Seattle: University of Washington Press, 1968.

A collection of short essays on aspects pertaining to both children's theater and creative drama; covers a wide range of topics; excellent for background reading.

Slade, Peter. *Child Drama.* New York: Philosophical Library, 1955.

Slade offers the British point of view about dramatic play. His work contains some extremely worthwhile information about early childhood and the beginnings of play.

Spolin, Viola. *Improvisation for the Theater.* Evanston, Illinois: Northwestern University Press, 1963.

One of the finest contemporary sources for information about improvisation. The author is an established authority on this aspect of dramatics. Although many of the exercises are intended for formal dramatic work, they are easily adaptable to classroom and stage work in creative drama. A virtual goldmine of suggestions.

Taylor, Loren E. *Pantomime and Pantomime Games.* Minneapolis: Burgess Publishing Company, 1966.

A very practical how-to-do-it book; offers many different activities suitable for use in the classroom with most ages.

Way, Brian. *Development through Drama.* New York: Humanities Press, 1967.

A compendium of activities and knowledge about the many uses of creative drama at all grade levels. The author draws heavily on his own experiences, and the book has the ring of authenticity. Especially valuable are the suggestions for beginning activities and for exercises which involve movement, the senses, and the emotions. Available in paperback.

Appendixes

Appendix A
Suggested Outline of Content in a Creative Dramatics Course on the College Level

The outline for a creative dramatics course should serve as a guide to the first of three courses required for a creative dramatics major. The two courses which follow should emphasize more individual guidance by students with classmates and with children. Students majoring in creative dramatics should be well grounded in theater background and should be required to take courses in introduction to the theater, dramatic literature, storytelling, and children's theater. The outline presented here emphasizes participation, discussion, and evaluation.

I. Introduction to Creative Dramatics
    A. Definition, nature, and philosophy.
    B. History of the theater, with emphasis on the relation of children's drama to the mainstreams of dramatic art.
    C. Definitions and interpretations of related terms.
    D. Objectives and purposes of creative dramatics.
    E. Values of creative dramatics for children, teacher or leader, and for community and society.
    F. Application of educational principles to creative drama.
    G. Requirements of the creative dramatics leader.

II. Drama as an Art
    A. In the school curriculum (language arts and literature, social sciences, integrated studies, choral reading).
    B. Outside the curriculum (recreation, religious education, etc.).

III. Introduction to Basic Guidance Techniques
    A. Discussion of the nature, needs, interests, and aptitudes of each level (preschool, lower elementary, upper elementary, junior high school, high school).

165

B. Discussion of and participation in creative rhythms (ensemble movement and pantomimes; individual movement and pantomimes; exploring musical materials).

C. Discussion of and participation in dramatic play (motivation techniques; organization of ideas; creative guidance techniques).

IV. Introduction to Creative Guidance Techniques in Story Dramatization

A. Analysis of dramatic elements and story construction (selecting, preparing, motivating, and presenting a story).

B. Analysis of creative guidance techniques (building the story with characterization, scenes, plot, interaction, and dialogue).

C. Analysis of evaluation techniques (evaluating characterization and basic dramatic elements, imagination of interpretation, cooperation, sincerity in style and expression).

D. Analysis of guidance techniques in creating a play from an entire story.

V. Utilization of Role Playing and Sociodrama

A. Applications of role playing (sources of material, relationship to personal needs).

B. Applications of sociodrama (distinctions from role playing, sources of material, guidance application).

VI. Organization of Physical Aspects of Creative Dramatics Program

A. Discussion of space, optimum class size, length of sessions, number of sessions, adult observers, public relations.

B. Parent education (possible carry-over to parental guidance and application).

Adapted from Richard G. Adams, "Composite Course Outlines for Children's Theatre and Creative Dramatics at the College Level," *Children's Theatre and Creative Dramatics,* ed. Geraldine B. Siks and Hazel Dunnington (Seattle: University of Washington Press, 1961), pp. 229-33.

Appendix B
Drama and Teacher Education

The following items suggest areas which might be included in a new curriculum for teachers who intend to use drama as an integral part of their teaching.

Academic Study and Experiences (not in order of importance)

1. Birth and origins of saga, myth, legend, folklore; varying attitudes to and uses of them in different societies.
2. Differences in dramatic form: e.g., tragic, comic, didactic, absurd, dramatic play.
3. Group dynamics.
4. Anthropological studies of the place of theater and drama.
5. Understanding of play and elaboration procedures.
6. Child development. The stages of "dramatic growth." Individual and group needs.
7. Motivations in learning.
8. History of educational drama in formal learning situations— not only in Western schools, but in Eastern cultures as well.
9. Analysis of types of confrontations which create tension.
10. Mental health and the role of drama in therapy.
11. Sociology—particularly in the areas of groups and methods of communication.

Practical Experiences (not in order of importance)

1. Production without "producing"—text, novel, play.
2. Self-discovery of teacher-type and resultant weaknesses and strengths.

3. Harnessing children's drama impulse to the classroom group situation.
4. Handling groups of all sizes in all sorts of spaces.
5. Skills of using tape recorders, lighting, and filming creatively.
6. Understanding relationships between movement, language, architecture, sculpture.
7. Collecting sources and resources.
8. Relationship of drama and other subjects.
9. Learning to "focus" for groups.
10. Studies in observation and analysis of self and others.
11. Ability to classify in the ongoing situation.
12. Grasp of and skills in the total signaling process in teaching.
13. A delicate understanding of verbal signaling; skill in the spoken word—choice of language, volume, and modulation.
14. Skill in handling tension and confrontation.
15. Skill in making plans which allow opportunities rather than creating rigid frameworks.
16. Learning to receive and to listen.
17. Skills of recovery and rehabilitation.

From Dorothy Heathcote, "Training Needs for the Future," a paper from *Drama in Education I: The Annual Survey,* edited by John Hodgson and Martin Banham (Sir Isaac Pitman & Sons, Ltd., London, 1972), pp. 81-83. Reprinted by permission of the publishers.

A Selected Bibliography

Abt, Clark C. "Education Is Child's Play." In *Inventing Education for the Future,* edited by Werner Z. Hirsch. San Francisco: Chandler Publishing Co., 1967.

_____. "Games and Simulation." Paper presented at the Abingdon Conference on "New Directions in Individualizing Instruction," April 1967.

Adams, Richard G. "Composite Course Outlines for Children's Theatre and Creative Dramatics at the College Level." In *Children's Theatre and Creative Dramatics,* edited by Geraldine B. Siks and Hazel Dunnington. Seattle: University of Washington Press, 1961.

American Educational Theatre Association. *Directory of American Colleges and Universities Offering Training in Children's Theatre and Creative Dramatics.* Rev. ed. Washington: American Educational Theatre Association, 1963.

Atkinson, Claudene D. "A New Approach: Drama in the Classroom." *English Journal* 60 (October 1971): 947-56.

Aubert, Charles. *The Art of Pantomime.* Translated by Edith Sears. New York: Henry Holt and Co., 1927.

Ausubel, David P. "Creativity, General Creative Abilities, and the Creative Individual." *Psychology in the Schools* 1 (October 1964): 344-47.

Ayllon, Maurie, and Snyder, Susan. "Behavioral Objectives in Creative Dramatics." *Journal of Educational Research* 62 (April 1969): 355-59.

Barbato, Lewis. "Drama Therapy." *Sociometry* 8 (August-November 1945): 396-98.

Barnes, Douglas, ed. *Drama in the English Classroom.* Urbana, Illinois: National Council of Teachers of English, 1968.

Barnfield, Gabriel. *Creative Drama in the Schools.* New York: Hart Publishing Co., 1968.

Barron, Frank. "Creativity: What Research Says about It." *NEA Journal* 50 (March 1961): 17-19.

Belo, Jane. "Balinese Children's Drawing." In *Childhood in Contemporary Cultures,* edited by Margaret Mead and Martha Wolfenstein, pp. 52-69. Chicago: University of Chicago Press, 1955.

Berger, Peter L. *Invitation to Sociology: A Humanistic Perspective.* Garden City, New York: Doubleday & Company, Anchor Books, 1963.

Bertram, Jean. "Creative Dramatics in the School." *Elementary English* 35 (December 1958): 515-18.

Birdwhistell, Ray L. "Background to Kinesics." *Etc.* 13 (Autumn 1955): 10-48.

____. *Kinesics and Context: Essays on Body Motion Communication.* Philadelphia: University of Pennsylvania Press, 1970.

Bishop, Richard. "Thats What Happen." In *Classroom Practices in Teaching English, 1971-72: Through a Glass Darkly,* edited by Edward R. Fagan and Jean Vandell, p. 18. Urbana, Illinois: National Council of Teachers of English, 1971.

Blackmur, R. P. "Language as Gesture." In *Language as Gesture: Essays in Poetry,* pp. 3-24. New York: Harcourt, Brace and World, 1952.

Board of Education (Great Britain). *Report on Primary Schools.* London: Her Majesty's Stationer's Office, 1931.

Bodwin, Shirley. "How We Banish Fears at Our House." *Parents' Magazine* 29 (August 1954): 34.

Boocock, Sarane S., and Coleman, James S. "Games with Simulated Environments in Learning." *Sociology of Education* 39 (Summer 1966): 215-36.

Borton, Terry. *Reach, Touch, and Teach.* New York: McGraw-Hill Book Co., 1970.

Boyd, Gertrude. "Role Playing." *Social Education* 21 (October 1969): 267-69.

Brack, Kenneth. "Creative Dramatics: Why? How? When?" *Elementary English* 36 (December 1959): 565-67.

Brewbaker, James M. "Simulation Games and the English Teacher." *English Journal* 61 (January 1972): 104-09.

Bristow, William H. "Sociometry, Sociodrama and the Curriculum." *Sociatry* 2 (April-August 1948): 73-74.

Brown, Corinne. *Creative Drama in the Lower School.* New York: D. Appleton and Co., 1929.

Brown, George I. *Human Teaching for Human Learning: An Introduction to Confluent Education.* New York: Viking Press, 1971.

____. "Teaching Creativity to Teachers and Others." *Journal of Teacher Education* 21 (Summer 1970): 210-16.

Burger, Isabel. *Creative Play Acting.* 2nd ed. New York: Ronald Press Co., 1966.

Calabria, Frances R. "The Why of Creative Dramatics." *Instructor* 77 (August 1967): 182.

Carlson, Bernice Wells, and Ginglend, David R. *Play Activities for the Retarded Child.* New York: Abingdon Press, 1961.

Chambers, Dewey W. *Storytelling and Creative Drama.* Dubuque, Iowa: Wm. C. Brown Co., 1970.

Chambers, Robert. *Creative Dramatics: Learning or Play?* Unpublished master's thesis, Ohio State University, 1956.

Chesler, Mark, and Fox, Robert. *Role-Playing Methods in the Classroom.* Teacher Resource Booklets on Classroom Social Relations and Learning. Chicago: Science Research Associates, 1966.

Chorpenning, Charlotte Barrows. *Twenty-One Years with Children's Theatre.* Anchorage, Kentucky: Children's Theatre Press, 1954.

Christensen, J. A. "School Drama." *Media & Methods* 8 (January 1972): 33.

Clark, C. H. *Brainstorming.* Garden City, New York: Doubleday & Co., 1958.

Coggin, Philip A. *The Uses of Drama.* New York: George Braziller, 1956.

Cohen, Stewart. "Creativity: An Implicit Goal in Education." *School and Society* 99 (March 1971): 174-76.

Cole, Natalie Robinson. *The Arts in the Classroom.* New York: John Day Co., 1940.

_____. "Exploring Psychodrama at Fifth Grade Level." *Sociatry* 2 (December-March 1948): 55-57.

Corsini, Raymond J. *Role Playing in Psychotherapy.* Chicago: Aldine Publishing Co., 1966.

Craddock, Myrtle. "Creative Dramatics for 9, 10, 11 Year Olds." *Childhood Education* 29 (January 1953): 230-34.

Creber, J. W. Patrick. *Sense and Sensitivity: The Philosophy and Practice of English Teaching.* London: University of London Press, 1965.

Crosby, Muriel. "Creative Dramatics as a Developmental Process." *Elementary English* 33 (January 1956): 13-18.

Crystal, Josie. "Role-playing in a Troubled Class." *Elementary School Journal* 69 (January 1969): 169-79.

Cullum, Albert. *Push Back the Desks.* New York: Citation Press, 1967.

Dearborn, Ned Harland. *The Oswego Movement in American Education.* Teachers College Contributions to Education, No. 183. New York: Columbia University, 1925.

DeNeler, Emmie. "The Central Point of the Platoon School." *Platoon School* (December-February 1930-31): 153-56.

Dennison, George. *The Lives of Children.* New York: Random House, 1969.

Dewey, John. *Construction and Criticism.* The First Davies Memorial Lecture, delivered February 25, 1930, for the Institute of Arts and Sciences. New York: Columbia University Press, 1930.

Downs, Genevieve R., and Pitkanen, Allan M. "Therapeutic Dramatics for Delinquent Boys." *Clearing House* 27 (March 1953): 423-26.

"Drama Is the Key." *Times* (London) *Educational Supplement.* No. 2716 (June 9, 1967): 1937.

Duke, Charles R. "Creative Dramatics: A Natural for the Multiple Elective Program." *Virginia English Bulletin* 21 (Winter 1971): 9.

____. "Livening Up Nonfiction." *NEA Journal* 57 (February 1968): 63.

____. "Space and Body English: Keys to Speech Evaluation." In *Classroom Practices in Teaching English, 1972-73: Measure for Measure,* edited by Allen Berger and Blanche Hope Smith, pp. 70-74. Urbana, Illinois: National Council of Teachers of English, 1972.

Dumas, Wayne. "Role Playing: Effective Technique in the Teaching of History." *Clearing House* 44 (April 1970): 468-70.

Durland, Frances Caldwell. *Creative Dramatics for Children.* Yellow Springs, Ohio: Antioch Press, 1952.

Ebbitt, Paul F. "Drama for Slow Learners." *English Journal* 52 (November 1963): 624-26.

Eek, Nat. "Theatre, Children's." In *The Encyclopedia of Education,* edited by Lee C. Deighton, vol. 9, pp. 227-30. New York: Macmillan Co., 1971.

Eliasoph, Eugene. "Concepts and Techniques of Role Playing and Role Training Utilizing Psychodramatic Methods in Group Therapy with Adolescent Drug Addicts." *Group Psychotherapy* 8 (December 1955): 308-15.

Fast, Julius. *Body Language.* New York: Pocket Books, 1971.

Featherstone, Joseph. "How Children Learn." *New Republic* 157 (September 2, 1967): 17-21.

Ferebee, J. D. "Learning Form through Creative Expression." *Elementary English* 27 (January 1950): 73-78.

Fertik, Marian I. "A Crescendo: Creative Dramatics in Philadelphia." *Wilson Library Bulletin* 42 (October 1968): 160-64.

Fitchett, Carolyn. "An English Unit: Chamber Theatre Technique." Newton, Massachusetts: Curriculum Resources Group, 1966.

Fliegler, A. Lois. "Play Acting with the Mentally Retarded." *Exceptional Children* 19 (November 1952): 56-60.

Frazier, Clifford. *Discovery in Drama.* New York: Paulist Press, 1969.

Friedrich, Dick, and Kuester, David. *It's Mine and I'll Write It That Way.* New York: Random House, 1972.

Fromm, Eric. *Escape from Freedom.* New York: Rinehart and Co., 1947.

Gillies, Emily. "We Believe." In *Creative Dramatics,* edited by Margaret Rasmussen. Washington: Association for Childhood Education International, 1961.

Gordon, William J. J. *Synectics.* New York: Harper and Brothers, 1961.

Government of Northern Ireland Ministry of Education. *Provision for Primary Schools.* Belfast, Northern Ireland: Her Majesty's Stationer's Office, 1956.

Grambs, Jean D. Review of *Role Playing for Social Values,* by Fannie R. Shaftel. *Teachers College Record* 70 (October 1968): 92.

Grambs, Jean D., and Kinney, Lucien B. "Sociodrama in High School Classes." *Social Education* 12 (December 1948): 341-43.

Graubard, Paul S. "Pantomime: Another Language." *Elementary English* 37 (May 1960): 302-06.

Gray, Farnum. "The Pennsylvania Advancement School." In *Radical*

School Reform, edited by Ronald Gross and Beatrice Gross, pp. 306-21. New York: Simon & Schuster, 1969.

Greenleaf, Walter J. "Sociodrama as a Guidance Technique." *California Journal of Secondary Education* 26 (February 1951): 71-75.

Haaga, Agnes. "Recommended Training for Creative Dramatics Leaders." In *Children's Theatre and Creative Dramatics,* edited by Geraldine B. Siks and Hazel Dunnington. Seattle: University of Washington Press, 1961.

Haas, Robert B. "Implications and Recommendations for Educational Practice: Sociodrama in Education." *Sociatry* 2 (December-March 1948): 232-41.

Hall, Edward Twitchell. *The Silent Language.* New York: Doubleday & Co., 1959.

Harris, Peter, ed. *Drama in Education.* London: Bodley Head, 1967.

Hartman, Gertrude, and Shumaker, Ann, eds. *Creative Expression.* New York: John Day Co., 1932; 2nd ed. Milwaukee: E. M. Hale and Co., 1939.

Hawkes, Geoffrey. "Dramatic Work for Backward Children." In *English for the Rejected* by David Holbrook, pp. 247-53. London: Cambridge University Press, 1964.

Hayes, Eloise. "Expanding the Child's World through Drama and Movement." *Childhood Education* 47 (April 1971): 360-67.

Heathcote, Dorothy. "Drama." In *Challenge and Change in the Teaching of English,* edited by Arthur Daigon and Ronald LaConte, pp. 138-46. Boston: Allyn & Bacon, 1971.

_____. "How Does Drama Serve Thinking, Talking, and Writing?" *Elementary English* 47 (December 1970): 1077-81.

_____. "Improvisation." In *Drama in Education,* edited by Peter Harris. London: Bodley Head, 1967.

_____. "Training Needs for the Future." In *Drama in Education I: The Annual Survey,* edited by John Hodgson and Martin Banham. New York: Pitman Publishing Corp., 1972.

Henry, Mabel Wright. "The Need for Creative Experiences in Oral Language." In *Creative Experiences in Oral Language,* edited by Mabel Wright Henry. Urbana, Illinois: National Council of Teachers of English, 1967.

Hirsch, Werner Z., ed. *Inventing Education for the Future.* San Francisco: Chandler Publishing Co., 1967.

Hodgson, J., and Richards, E. *Improvisation.* London: Methuen and Co., 1966.

Hodgson, John, and Banham, Martin, eds. *Drama in Education I: The Annual Survey.* New York: Pitman Publishing Corp., 1972.

Hoetker, James. *Dramatics and the Teaching of Literature.* Urbana, Illinois: National Council of Teachers of English, 1969.

_____. *Students as Audiences: An Experimental Study of the Relationships between Classroom Study of Drama and Attendance at the Theatre.* Research Report No. 11. Urbana, Illinois: National Council of Teachers of English, 1971.

Hoffer, Eric. *The Ordeal of Change.* New York: Harper & Row, 1963.

Holbrook, David. "Creativity in the English Programme." In *Creativity in English,* edited by Geoffrey Summerfield. Urbana, Illinois: National Council of Teachers of English, 1968.

_____ . *English for Maturity.* London: Cambridge University Press, 1961.

_____ . *English for the Rejected.* London: Cambridge University Press, 1964.

Hutchinson, Eliot Dole. *How to Think Creatively.* New York: Abingdon-Cokesbury Press, 1949.

Huxley, Aldous. "Education on the Non-Verbal Level." In *Contemporary Educational Psychology: Selected Essays,* edited by Richard M. Jones, pp. 41-60. New York: Harper & Row, 1967.

Iverson, William J. "The Lively Arts of Language in the Elementary Schools." In *The Discovery of English,* 1971 NCTE Distinguished Lectures, pp. 81-96. Urbana, Illinois: National Council of Teachers of English, 1971.

Jespersen, Otto. *Essentials of English Grammar.* New York: Henry Holt and Co., 1933.

Johnson, Kenneth R. "Black Kinesics: Some Non-Verbal Communication Patterns in the Black Culture." *Florida FL Reporter* 9 (Spring-Fall 1971): 17.

Jones, Catherine J. "The Creativity Problem." *Illinois School Journal* 51 (Spring 1971): 2-9.

Kahn, Samuel. *Psychodrama Explained.* New York: Philosophical Library, 1964.

Kase, Judith B. "Theatre Resources for Youth in New Hampshire." *Educational Theatre Journal* 21 (May 1969): 205-13.

Kaufman, Ben. "Improvised Dialogue in the Junior High School." *English Journal* 28 (April 1939): 288-95.

Keyes, George I. "Creative Dramatics and the Slow Learner." *English Journal* 54 (February 1965): 81-84.

Klein, Alan F. *Role Playing in Leadership Training and Group Problem Solving.* New York: Association Press, 1956.

Klietsch, Ronald G., et al. *Directory of Educational Simulations, Learning Games and Didactic Units.* St. Paul, Minnesota: Instructional Simulations, 1969.

Laban, Rudolf. *The Mastery of Movement.* Rev. ed. Boston: Plays, Inc., 1971.

Lee, Jennie. *Drama.* Department of Education and Science Education Survey 2. London: Her Majesty's Stationery Office, 1968.

Lee, Joseph. *Play in Education.* New York: Macmillan Co., 1929.

Levy, Ronald B. "Psychodrama and the Philosophy of Cultural Education." *Sociatry* 2 (December-March 1948): 225-34.

Lewis, Richard. "Do Children Have a Culture of Their Own?" *This Magazine Is About Schools* 5 (Winter 1971): 60-96.

Lippitt, Rosemary. "The Auxiliary Chair Technique." *Group Psychotherapy,* No. 11. (1958): 8-23.

_____ . "Psychodrama in the Home." *Sociatry* 1 (June 1947): 145-67.

Lowenfeld, Viktor. "Current Research on Creativity." *NEA Journal* 47 (November 1958): 538-40.

Lowenfeld, Viktor, and Brittain, W. Lambert. *Creative and Mental Growth*. 4th ed. New York: Macmillan Co., 1964.

Ludwig, Charlotte. *The Effect of Creative Dramatics Activities upon the Articulation Skills of Kindergarten Children*. Unpublished master's thesis, University of Pittsburgh, 1955.

Magers, Joan. "The Role-playing Technique in Teaching a Novel." *English Journal* 57 (October 1968): 990-91.

Marksberry, Mary Lee. *Foundation of Creativity*. New York: Harper & Row, 1963.

McCalib, Paul T. "Intensifying the Literary Experience through Role-playing." *English Journal* 57 (January 1968): 41-46.

McCarroll, Jessie M., and Poley, Irwin C. "All the News and No Print: An Adaptation of the Living Newspaper." *English Journal* 29 (September 1940): 572-76.

McCaslin, Nellie. *Creative Dramatics in the Classroom*. New York: David McKay Co., 1968.

McIntyre, Barbara M. "Creative Dramatics." *Education* 79 (April 1959): 495-98.

_____. "Creative Dramatics in Programs for Exceptional Children." In *Children's Theatre and Creative Dramatics,* edited by Geraldine B. Siks and Hazel Dunnington. Seattle: University of Washington Press, 1961.

_____. "The Effect of Creative Activities on the Articulation Skills of Children." *Speech Monograph* (1958): 42-48.

_____. *The Effects of a Program of Creative Activities upon the Articulation Skills of Adolescent and Pre-Adolescent Children with Speech Disorders*. Unpublished doctoral dissertation, University of Pittsburgh, 1957.

_____. *Informal Dramatics: A Language Arts Activity for the Special Pupil*. Pittsburgh: Stanwix House, 1963.

McIntyre, Barbara M., and McWilliams, Betty Jane. "Creative Dramatics in Speech Correction." *Journal of Speech and Hearing Disorders* 24 (August 1959): 275-79.

McLuhan, Marshall, and Fiore, Quentin. *The Medium Is the Massage*. New York: Bantam Books, 1967.

Mearns, Hughes. *The Creative Adult*. New York: Doubleday, Doran and Co., 1940.

_____. "The Creative Spirit and Its Significance for Education." In *Creative Expression,* edited by Gertrude Hartman and Ann Shumaker. New York: John Day Co., 1932.

Meersman, Roger. "Creative Dramatics for the Mentally Ill Adult." *Speech Teacher* 18 (January 1969): 58-64.

Meir, Richard L. "Simulations for Transmitting Concepts of Social Organization." In *Inventing Education for the Future,* edited by Werner Z. Hirsch. San Francisco: Chandler Publishing Co., 1967.

Merrill, John. "Dramatics: A Mode of Study." *Progressive Education* 8 (January 1931): 58-70.

Merrill, John, and Fleming, Martha. *Playmaking and Plays*. New York: Macmillan Co., 1930.

Michael, William B., ed. *Teaching for Creative Endeavor*. Bloomington: Indiana University Press, 1968.

Ministry of Education (Great Britain). *Drama in the Schools of Wales*. London: Her Majesty's Stationer's Office, 1954.

Moffett, James. *Drama: What Is Happening*. Urbana, Illinois: National Council of Teachers of English, 1967.

____. *A Student-Centered Language Arts Curriculum, Grades K-13: A Handbook for Teachers*. Boston: Houghton Mifflin Co., 1973.

Mooney, Ross L., and Razik, Taher A., eds. *Explorations in Creativity*. New York: Harper & Row, 1967.

Moreno, Jacob L. *Psychodrama*. New York: Beacon House, 1946.

____. *The Theatre of Spontaneity*. New York: Beacon House, 1947.

Morrison, Eleanor Shelton, and Foster, Virgil E. "The Use of Creative Drama with Children." *International Journal of Religious Education* 40 (September 1963): 4-9.

Moskowitz, Estelle. "Dramatics as an Educational Approach to the Mentally Handicapped." *Quarterly Journal of Speech* 28 (April 1942): 215-19.

Moustakas, Clark. "Creativity and Conformity in Education." In *Explorations in Creativity*, edited by Ross L. Mooney and Taher A. Razik. New York: Harper & Row, 1967.

Muller, Herbert J. *The Uses of English*. New York: Holt, Rinehart and Winston, 1967.

Munch, Theo W. "A Sociodramatic Slant to Science Teaching." *Science Education* 37 (December 1953): 318-20.

Murphy, Gardner. "The Process of Creative Thinking." *Educational Leadership* 14 (October 1956): 11-15.

National Education Association. *Unfinished Stories for Use in the Classroom*. Washington: National Education Association, n.d.

Nau, Elizabeth S. "Making Marionettes for the Classroom." *Elementary English* 29 (January 1952): 19-25.

Neill, A. S. "Each His Own Dramatist: Spontaneous Acting for Children." *Times* (London) *Educational Supplement* (December 2, 1960): 752.

Northwestern University. *Annual Announcement: School of Speech, 1926*. Northwestern University Bulletin, vol. 25, no. 39. Evanston, Illinois: Northwestern University.

____. *Annual Announcement: School of Speech, 1938-1939*. Northwestern University Bulletin, vol. 38, no. 39. Evanston, Illinois: Northwestern University.

Osten, Gwen. "Structure in Creativity." *Elementary English* 46 (April 1969): 438-43.

Parker, Francis W. *Talks on Pedagogics*. New York: A. S. Barnes and Co., 1894.

Patrick, Catherine. *What Is Creative Thinking?* New York: Philosophical Library, 1955.

Peluso, Joseph L. *A Survey of the Status of Theatre in United States High Schools*. Washington: U.S. Department of Health, Education, and Welfare, 1970.

Pemberton-Billing, R. N., and Clegg, A. B. *Teaching Drama*. London:

University of London Press; New York: International Publications Service, 1965.

Perry, Harold J. "Living Newspaper." *English Journal* 39)January 1950): 11-15.

Pierini, Patricia Marie. *Application of Creative Dramatics to Speech Therapy.* Unpublished master's thesis, Stanford University, 1956.

Piers, E. V., Daniels, J. M., and Quackenbush, J. F. "The Identification of Creativity in Adolescents." *Journal of Educational Psychology* 51 (1960): 346-51.

Pitcole, Marcia. "Black Boy and Role Playing: A Scenario for Reading Success." *English Journal* 57 (November 1968): 1140-42.

Popovich, James E. "Considerations in the Teaching of Creative Dramatics." *Speech Teacher* 8 (November 1959): 283-87.

———. *A Study of Significant Contributions to the Development of Creative Dramatics in American Education.* Unpublished doctoral dissertation, Northwestern University, 1955.

Potter, David, and Andersen, Martin P. "Role-Playing in Discussion." In *Discussion: A Guide to Effective Practice,* pp. 129-48. Belmont, California: Wadsworth Publishing Co., 1963.

Presler, Frances. "Developing Dramatics in the Public Schools." *Progressive Education* 8 (January 1931): 43-46.

Putnam, Helen. "Faculty Discussions of School Plays." *Francis W. Parker Studies in Education* 1 (1912): 75.

Rapp, Marvin. "The Brainstorming Attitude." *School Arts* 59 (June 1969): 5-8.

Rasmussen, Margaret, ed. *Creative Dramatics.* Washington: Association for Childhood Education International, 1961.

Rogers, Carl. *Freedom to Learn.* Columbus, Ohio: Charles E. Merrill Publishing Co., 1969.

Rothstein, Jerome H., ed. *Mental Retardation: Readings and Resources.* New York: Holt, Rinehart and Winston, 1961.

Rubin, Louis J. "Creativity in the Curriculum." In *Teaching for Creative Endeavor,* edited by William B. Michael. Bloomington: Indiana University Press, 1968.

Ruesch, Jurgen, and Kees, Weldon. *Nonverbal Communication: Notes on the Visual Perception of Human Relations.* Berkeley: University of California Press, 1956.

Rugg, Harold, and Shumaker, Ann. *The Child-Centered School.* New York: World Book Co., 1928.

Sawyer, Ruth. *The Way of the Storyteller.* London: Bodley Head, 1962.

Sayre, Gwenda. *Creative Miming.* London: Herbert Jenkins, 1959.

Schactel, E. G. *Metamorphosis: On the Development of Affect, Perception, Attention, and Memory.* New York: Basic Books, 1959.

Schattner, Regina. *Creative Dramatics for Handicapped Children.* New York: John Day Co., 1967.

Schools, Leo J. "Lifeboat." *Media & Methods* 7 (September 1971): 86.

Schutz, William C. *Joy.* New York: Grove Press, 1967.

Schwartz, Dorothy T. "Development of the Children's Theatre Conference." In *Children's Theatre and Creative Dramatics,* edited by Geraldine B. Siks and Hazel Dunnington. Seattle: University of Washington Press, 1961.

Schwartz, Sheila. "New Methods in Creative Dramatics." *Elementary English* 36 (November 1959): 484-87.

Scofield, Robert W. "A Creative Climate." *Educational Leadership* 18 (October 1960): 5-6.

Selden, Samuel. *First Steps in Acting.* New York: F. S. Crofts and Co., 1947.

Senderowitz, Ralph B. "How One Community Uses Creative Dramatics—With Emphasis on the Ten-to-Twelve-Year Olds' Program." In *Creative Dramatics,* edited by Margaret Rasmussen. Washington: Association for Childhood Education International, 1961.

Shaftel, Fannie R. *Role Playing for Social Values.* Englewood Cliffs, New Jersey: Prentice-Hall, 1967.

Shaftel, Fannie R., and Shaftel, George. "Role-playing as a Learning Method for Disadvantaged Children." *School and Society* 94 (December 24, 1966): 494-98.

_____. *Role Playing the Problem Story.* New York: National Conference of Christians and Jews, Commission on Educational Organizations, 1952.

_____. *Words and Actions: Role-Playing Photo-problems for Young Children.* New York: Holt, Rinehart and Winston, 1967.

Sheldon, Edward Austin. *A Manual of Elementary Instruction.* New York: Scribner, Armstrong and Co., 1874.

Shelhammer, Lois B. "Solving Personal Problems through Sociodrama." *English Journal* 38 (November 1949): 503-05.

Sheridan, Marion. "Creative Language Experiences in High School." *English Journal* 49 (November 1960): 563-69.

Shoobs, Nahum E. *Psychodrama in the Schools.* New York: Beacon House, 1944.

Shuman, R. Baird. "Adjectives on Tape." *Audio-Visual Guide* 21 (November 1954): 29-30.

Shuman, R. Baird, and Sublett, Henry L., Jr. "Home Study as an Aid to Learning." *Western Carolina University Journal of Education* 3 (Fall 1971): 17-21.

Side, Ronald. "Creative Drama." *Elementary English* 46 (April 1969): 431-35.

Sievers, W. David. "Creative Dramatics as a Force in Social Adjustment." *California Journal of Secondary Education* 28 (November 1953): 393-97.

Siks, Geraldine Brain. "An Appraisal of Creative Dramatics." *Educational Theatre Journal* 17 (December 1965): 329.

_____. *Children's Literature for Dramatization.* New York: Harper & Row, 1964.

_____. *Creative Dramatics: An Art for Children.* New York: Harper and Brothers, 1958.

Siks, Geraldine Brain, and Dunnington, Hazel B., eds. *Children's Theatre and Creative Dramatics*. Seattle: University of Washington Press, 1961.

Silberman, Charles E. *Crisis in the Classroom*. New York: Random House, 1970.

Simon, Marianne P., and Simon, Sidney B. "Dramatic Improvisation: Path to Discovery." *English Journal* 54 (April 1965): 323-27.

Slade, Peter. *Child Drama*. New York: Philosophical Library, 1955.

Smith, P., ed. *Creativity*. New York: Hastings House, 1959.

Spolin, Viola. *Improvisation for the Theater*. Evanston, Illinois: Northwestern University Press, 1963.

Squire, James R., and Applebee, Roger K. *High School English Instruction Today*. New York: Appleton-Century-Crofts, 1968.

_____. *Teaching English in the United Kingdom*. Urbana, Illinois: National Council of Teachers of English, 1969.

Summerfield, Geoffrey, ed. *Creativity in English*. Urbana, Illinois: National Council of Teachers of English, 1968.

Swaminathan, Mina. *Drama in Schools*. New Delhi: National Council of Educational Research and Training, 1968.

Taylor, I. A. "The Nature of Creative Process." In *Creativity*, edited by P. Smith. New York: Hastings House, 1959.

Taylor, Loren E. *Pantomime and Pantomime Games*. Minneapolis: Burgess Publishing Co., 1965.

_____. *Puppetry, Marionettes and Shadow Plays*. Minneapolis: Burgess Publishing Co., 1965.

Thomas, George I., and Crescimbeni, Joseph. *Individualizing Instruction in the Elementary School*. New York: Random House, 1967.

Toffler, Alvin. *Future Shock*. New York: Random House, 1970.

Torrance, E. Paul. *Encouraging Creativity in the Classroom*. Dubuque, Iowa: Wm. C. Brown Co., 1970.

_____. *Guiding Creative Talent*. Englewood Cliffs, New Jersey: Prentice-Hall, 1962.

_____. "Nurture of Creative Talents." In *Explorations in Creativity*, edited by Ross L. Mooney and Taher A. Razik. New York: Harper & Row, 1967.

_____. *Rewarding Creative Behavior*. Englewood Cliffs, New Jersey: Prentice-Hall, 1965.

Torrance, E. Paul, and Fortson, Laura R. "Creativity among Young Children and the Creative-Aesthetic Approach." *Education* 89 (September-October 1968): 27-30.

Traynor, Raymond. "Who Knows What Lurks in the Heart of an Old Philco." *Media & Methods* 7 (April 1971): 37.

Vaughan, M. S. "Creativity and Creative Teaching: A Reappraisal." *School and Society* 97 (April 1969): 230-32.

Viola, Ann. "Drama with and for Children: An Interpretation of Terms." *Educational Theatre Journal* 8 (May 1956): 139-42.

Walker, Kathrine Sorley. *Eyes on Mime*. New York: John Day Co., 1969.

Ward, Winifred. *Creative Dramatics for the Upper Grades and Junior High School.* New York: D. Appleton-Century Co., 1930.

____. "Creative Dramatics in the Elementary School." *Quarterly Journal of Speech* 28 (December 1942): 445-49.

____. "Creative versus Formal Dramatics." *Southern Speech Bulletin* 2 (March 1937): 4-6.

____. *Playmaking with Children.* New York: D. Appleton-Century Co., 1947.

____. *Theatre for Children.* New York: D. Appleton-Century Co., 1939.

Way, Brian. *Development through Drama.* London: Longman Group, 1967.

Wilson, John, and Robeck, Mildred C. "Creativity in the Very Young." In *Teaching for Creative Endeavor,* edited by William B. Michael. Bloomington: Indiana University Press, 1968.

Yates, Sr. Mary Clare. "Choose Your Environment." In *Lecture Alternatives in Teaching English,* edited by Stephen Judy, pp. 48-56. Ann Arbor: Michigan Council of Teachers of English, 1971.

York, Eleanor Chase. "Values to Children from Creative Dramatics." In *Children's Theatre and Creative Dramatics,* edited by Geraldine B. Siks and Hazel Dunnington. Seattle: University of Washington Press, 1961.

Zirbes, Laura. *Spurs to Creative Teaching.* New York: G. P. Putnam's Sons, 1959.

Zuckerman, David W., and Horn, Robert E. *The Guide to Simulation Games for Education and Training.* Cambridge, Massachusetts: Information Resources, Inc., 1970.

New NCTE Titles on Creative Dramatics

Creative Dramatics Handbook, edited by Harriet W. Ehrlich. Building on children's love of play-pretend, Philadelphia teachers have developed an affective curriculum which incorporates creative dramatics into the regular classroom day. The hundreds of suggestions in this handbook emerged from workshops held over the years to train teachers in creative dramatics. Included are ideas for dealing with creative dramatic techniques—sense memory, characterization, etc.—and specific activities using pantomime, word games, improvisation, etc. Fifty vivid photographs testify to Ehrlich's conviction that creative dramatics can help children develop language skills, express strong feelings, and know "the sweet taste of success." Bibliography on multimedia resources. 192 pp. Revised edition manufactured by NCTE for the School Board of Philadelphia, 1974. Stock No. 34457. $5.50 ($5.00).

Drama in Your Classroom, edited by Iris M. Tiedt. Using drama in the classroom poses theoretical and practical problems explored in these articles. Authors analyze successful examples of creative play and give specific suggestions on using creative dramatics as a teaching technique in regular instruction. Other authors share ideas for puppetry, pantomime, and story dramatization. Annotated bibliography. 48 pp. Articles from the January 1974 *Elementary English.* Stock No. 08538. $1.65 ($1.50); 20 or more, $1.00 each.

An Idea Book for Acting Out and Writing Language, K-8, by Gary L. Gerbrandt. Gerbrandt suggests ways to use small groups successfully and then offers ideas that he and his student teachers tested with small classroom groups. Included are ideas for acting out language (pantomime, guessing games, charades, improvisation); ideas for writing out language (unfinished sentences, fables); and ideas for writing down language (scrambled sentences, dictated sentences). More than 700 examples are separated by grade level, difficulty, and number of students required. 78 pp. 1974. Stock No. 03150. $3.95 ($3.50).

Prices in parentheses are members' prices.